The Swastika in the Sanctuary

RECOGNIZING AND COMBATING THE RISE

OF NEO-NAZI FALSE DOCTRINES IN THE CHURCH

Jaród Murphey

GLASS MOUNTAINS

PUBLISHERS

Glass Mountains Publishers

820 W Danforth Rd

Unit #476

Edmond, OK 73003

ISBN: 979-8-9933099-1-0

Dedicated to my father-in-law, Cameron,
a Baptist pastor who is a "noble Berean" in the truest sense.
His faithful exposition of the Word and His constant use of
Scripture to challenge and reason with me in our many
theological conversations has influenced my life and
worldview significantly and for the better. I pray that he
continues to preach the Word faithfully in and out of season.

Table of Contents

Chapter I: Wolves in Our Midst

Across the Western world, Christians are struggling with the pernicious revival of Neo-Nazi false doctrines that are stealing the hearts and minds of the next generation of young people, particularly young men. This movement, which largely started in the recesses of the dark web, is now becoming mainstream. Pastors, teachers, podcasters, and influencers now openly push violent anti-Jewish and pro-Hitler rhetoric. Young men who are your coworkers, family members, and fellow church members are increasingly being seduced and led astray by these lies.

Corey Mahler, a Maryville, Tennessee attorney and Christian teacher who hosts the Stone Choir podcast with tens of thousands of followers made a statement which perfectly illustrates the sentiments of many of these young men:

Adolf Hitler proclaimed his Christian faith publicly, repeatedly, and under extreme distress. He did so in his first address as Chancellor and in his last address as Führer. The reason that you are taught to hate him is precisely this: He was the last Christian prince who

1

tried — desperately — to save Christendom. Satan cannot have you practicing a true and living faith.[1]

Mahler, who has been greatly influential among young, disaffected, right-wing men, has not shied away from leading them down a violent path. In response to a Christian pastor stating, "Any form of Christianity that hates Jews is completely anti-Christ," Mahler commented, "Under Christian Nationalism, Zionism will be a capital offense."[2] Since millions of Christians in the United States hold to Zionism (the belief that the Jews have a right to their own nation), this policy advocated by Mahler would result in the largest genocide against Christians in history (under the banner of "Christian" Nationalism). Such murderous insanity is not surprising to those who are familiar with Mahler, however, since he previously proclaimed, "Genocide is a legitimate tool of statecraft, and the Christian prince may employ it when warranted."[3]

---

[1] Mahler, C. (2025, June 26). *Adolf Hitler proclaimed his Christian faith publicly, repeatedly, and under extreme distress. He did so in his first address as Chancellor...* [Post]. X. https://x.com/CoreyJMahler/status/1938371633179168768

[2] Mahler, C. (2025, June 30). *Under Christian Nationalism, Zionism will be a capital offense.* [Post]. X. https://x.com/CoreyJMahler/status/1939630267389391032

[3] Spencer, W. (2025, June 2). The Dangerous Secret Your Young Men Are Keeping: Neo-Nazi Thought Has Entered the Church. Christ Over

Despite being aware of Mahler's bloodthirsty propositions, thousands of young "Christian" men continue to soak up his teachings. "The first and fiercest punishment first on the Dispensationalist, second on the Jew,"[4] "It should be illegal — a capital crime — for non-Americans to possess a firearm on American soil. Blacks are not Americans,"[5] and, "We win down here — *and then we make the enemies of God suffer,*"[6] are just some of the vile teachings Mahler has sold to the growing number of men who are willing to listen to him.

Mahler is not the only snake injecting his venom into the church. Joel Webbon, Pastor of Covenant Bible Church in Georgetown, Texas and Christian political influencer who has encouraged others to follow Corey Mahler,[7] has taught, "I believe those of Jewish decent [sic] are generally marked

---

All.
https://christoverall.com/article/longform/the-dangerous-secret-your-young-men-are-keeping-neo-nazi-thought-has-entered-the-church/
[4] Ibid.
[5] Ibid.
[6] Ibid.
[7] Webbon, J. (2025, February 6). *Fantastic new list of people to follow just dropped.* [Post]. X.
https://x.com/rightresponsem/status/1887732543723565547

by subversion, deceit, and greed."[8] On another day, Webbon commented, "I don't even believe Ashkenazi Jews are the physical descendants of ancient Israel."[9] Additionally, Webbon taught,

> Judaism by nature, in its ideology and in its religion, is, I believe, parasitical. And, yes, I'm using the word parasitical. […] Yes, parasitical. I'm not calling each and every Jew parasitical. I'm not saying that. I'm saying Judaism, as an ideology and as a religion, I do believe is parasitical—that what it has done historically, throughout the ages, is typically go into other countries, other peoples, with other religions, and kind of cozy up, but not really for their benefit. Not a mutually beneficial relationship, but where they ultimately get far more out of the deal than the Christian nation does. Judaism has thrived on Christendom. If Christendom falls and the West falls, and Islam wins the day, Muslims will not play nice with Jews. They will be screwed. Jews need

---

[8] Webbon, J. (2025, June 25). *Alright, I've picked up quite a few new followers so I want to be completely forthright with where I stand…* [Post]. X. https://x.com/rightresponsem/status/1937932928589127742
[9] Webbon, J. (2025, July 15). *I understand your point: "God is *able to* graft them back in…" is not the same as "God *will* graft…* [Post]. X. https://x.com/rightresponsem/status/1945139291341877729

Christians. Christians do not need Jews. It is not a mutually beneficial relationship.[10]

Similarly, Brian Sauvé, Christian musician, influencer, and pastor of Refuge Church in Ogden, Utah, stated, "Jews have been deeply involved in the smutification of American media—from Hollywood to internet pornography to OnlyFans—and not just recently."[11] When pressed at a later date, Sauvé admitted that he has not been able to find any statistical evidence regarding how much of the porn industry is Jewish, but he still believes that Jews are disproportionately involved in architecting the industry anyways.[12] Eric Conn, co-pastor of the same church, rails against "Jewish Bolsheviks."[13]

---

[10] Unsupervised Woman Tweeting. (2024, December 2). *"Judaism, by nature, in its ideology and its religion is, I believe, parasitical. And yes, I'm using the word parasitical."....* [Post with video]. X.
https://x.com/HasBrainCanRead/status/1863642742481354851

[11] Sauvé, B. (2025, June 4). *The only reason that Jews are in pornography is that we think that Christ sucks. Catholicism sucks. We don't believe...* [Post]. X.
https://x.com/Brian_Sauve/status/1930301505661481450

[12] Sauvé, B. (2025, September 15). *It is very, very difficult to find accurate numbers on this issue. Nobody really centrally tracks it. What you can...* [Post]. X.
https://x.com/Brian_Sauve/status/1967656288428625966

[13] Upton, J. (2025, April 10). My Weekend with Christian Nationalists: Anti-Semitism and Baseless Hatred at the Christ is King Conference. First Fruits of Zion.
https://ffoz.org/messiah/articles/my-weekend-with-christian-nationalists

Michael Spangler, pastor of Piedmont Presbyterian Church in North Carolina and author of *Christian Race Realism*, teaches,

> We anti-Semites are not unmanly. Rather, we are hardened Christian warriors, bound by necessity to fight with all our might against the power of the world, the state, the devil, and indeed the church, all which are sick with godless love for Christ's sworn enemies, the Jews. In this fight we have lost favor, family, friends, work, fellowship, and ministry. And we have done so gladly, for the gain of a clean conscience and the favor of our Lord, and of his faithful servants. This is not at all unmanly.[14]

As dorky as this statement sounds, it was not made in satire. On their path of destruction, those who hate the Jews and love the doctrines of Nazism are willing to fight even the church. They hate the true church because the Head of the church, Christ, is a Jew, and He gives true members of His church love, not hatred, for the Jews (Romans 9:1-5).

---

[14] Spangler, M. (2025, March 7). True Manliness and Christian Anti-Semitism. Michael Spangler. https://spanglermt.substack.com/p/true-manliness-and-christian-anti

Another destructive Christian influencer, Candace Owens, who has millions of followers, has taught false conspiracy theories about the Jews. One of the most egregious of these deceptions is her variation of the medieval "blood-libel" claim that Jews abduct and murder Christian children, offering them as Passover sacrifices. Owens even implied that the state of Israel was founded to protect Jews who participated in these sacrifices and needed to flee from Christians who were opposed to it.[15] Such falsehoods inevitably lead impressionable young men to believe that it is urgent and imperative to stop the Jews from murdering children by any means necessary. If the doctrines of Nazism offer the solution, they will grasp at it.

Nicholas "Nick" Fuentes, a Catholic influencer with over 700,000 followers who is known for helping popularize the chant "Christ is King" which has been used as an anti-Jewish rallying cry, has taught some of the most ugly, perverted, and deranged things I have ever seen from a major public figure. For instance, when being taunted by his audience for being a "fakecel" (someone who says that they

---

[15] Prager, D. (2024, September 3). A Letter from Dennis Prager to Candace Owens. Pp. 1-2.
https://assets.ctfassets.net/qnesrjodfi80/4rR7bx8wnD4YcM06JiBp3l/36e46704f8d36e2fb6db3c79db3c88ee/a_letter_from_dennis_prager_to_candace_owens.pdf

are an involuntary celibate, despite having previous romantic encounters), Fuentes responded that, like Hitler, he did not want a relationship; instead, "All I want is revenge against my enemies and a total Aryan victory. [...] I'm just like Hitler."[16]

While playing a speech by Gavin Newsom, Democratic Governor of California, on his show, Nick Fuentes had the following comments:

> Aryan! Look at this Aryan. [...] Chad! Chad Gavin Newsom. If you don't like Gavin Newsom, you're kind of, like, gay. I just don't know what to tell you. Like, if you look at a handsome, sociopathic, tall, White man who, like, clearly has contempt for, like, those around him, and you don't like it because he's a Democrat, "Ugh, but he's a Democrat," like, there's something wrong with you. I don't know what else to say. "Ugh, but he's not a Republican! Ugh, he may be tall, White, handsome, sociopathic, with a beautiful White family and rich, but he's not a Republican!" Like, I don't know what to tell you. Like, you're

[16] Right Wing Watch. (2022, February 7). *After admitting he once kissed a girl in high school, the Groypers in Nick Fuentes' superchat taunted him for...* [Post]. X. https://x.com/RightWingWatch/status/1490738194974920710

retarded? You are gay? I don't know what to say. "But he's a Democrat!" Okay, and? And? You know people say they're, like, White nationalists and then they look at a, like, successful White guy and they're, like, "But he's a Democrat." Like, okay, so you're the worst White nationalist ever. You're the worst White nationalist ever![17]

In the years prior to the assassination of Christian, conservative, pro-Israel political influencer Charlie Kirk, Fuentes expressed his enmity towards Kirk on numerous occasions, including in August 2025, just one month before Kirk's murder.[18] On one such occasion, Fuentes stated,

> Let's focus all our firepower on Charlie Kirk. [...] Why are we doing this? It's because Charlie Kirk is a fake patriot, a fake Christian, and he hates his people. He's anti-White. This is our angle.[19]

---

[17] Peter. (2025, August 25). *BEHOLD! The Savant of Politics:* [Post with video of Nick Fuente's show]. X. https://x.com/peterpeccavi/status/1960140226694705200

[18] Max. (2025, September 12). *VIDEO: Nick Fuentes is deceiving you because he wants Charlie Kirk's audience.* [Post with videos of Nick Fuente's show]. X. https://x.com/MaxNordau/status/1966370863843877192

[19] Jingoistic Pig. (2025, September 13). *Here's Nick Fuentes sharing his thoughts on Charlie Kirk when he launched his campaign to disrupt TPUSA events (where he...* [Post with video clips of Nick Fuente's show]. X. https://x.com/jingoisticpig/status/1967019230236471512

We will examine more statements from Nick Fuentes later in this book. It is about this man that Pastor Joel Webbon stated, "Politically, he's a savant." On the same podcast that Webbon made this remark, he said that he has considered collaborating with Fuentes and likened Fuentes to great political influencers of old, like Henry Ford.[20] The founder of the Ford Motor Company is politically known, chiefly, for being a major promoter of antisemitism in the United States and for being beloved by Adolf Hitler, who said, "We look on Heinrich Ford as the leader of the growing Fascisti [Fascist] movement in America. We admire particularly his anti-Jewish policy."[21]

In addition to these false teachers, massive organizations with rapidly-growing membership like Patriot Front, which split out of the Neo-Nazi group Vanguard America,[22] are leading young men and their families astray.

---

[20] Duff, R. (2025, August 15). *Joel Webbon @rightresponsem called Nick Fuentes a political savant and likened him to Henry Ford If he wants to chase...* [Post with video from Joel Webbon's show]. X. https://x.com/ryancduff/status/1956447563625947519

[21] Antisemitism and Henry Ford's "The International Jew". (2025, May 14). United States Holocaust Memorial Museum, Washington, DC. https://encyclopedia.ushmm.org/content/en/article/antisemitism-and-henry-fords-international-jew

[22] Anti-Defamation League. (2017, July 18). Vanguard America. https://www.adl.org/resources/backgrounder/vanguard-america

Patriot Front is open only to Whites who are either Christians or European pagans,[23] prioritizes their disaster response efforts to help Whites "practically to the exclusion of all others,"[24] is anti-Israel,[25] and advocates for the creation and preservation of a White ethnostate in America.[26] Known for coordinating massive public marches of masked, uniformed members with flags, Patriot Front has been known to chant "blood and soil,"[27] a Nazi slogan. Despite the organization being falsely branded by many ignorant pundits as "feds" who were trying to make Republicans look bad leading up to the 2024 election, the organization has continued to operate and demonstrate in full force after the election of Donald Trump.

The Balaam Strategy

The threat posed to this generation of Christians by the wicked ideologies promoted by organizations like Patriot

---

[23] Jake Shields' Fight Back Podcast. (2024, December 22). *Patriot Front's Thomas Rousseau Explains Their Beliefs - Fight Back Ep. 36.* [Video]. YouTube. https://youtu.be/NcNlBDa1qgs?si=VJ3-GOMm-UwWjmJz&t=2921

[24] Ibid.

[25] Ibid.

[26] Patriot Front. (n.d.). The George Washington University Program on Extremism. https://extremism.gwu.edu/patriot-front

[27] Ibid.

Front and influencers like Corey Mahler, Joel Webbon, Candace Owens, and Nick Fuentes must not be minimized. The most perilous threat to Christianity has never been persecution by the world; rather, it has always been infiltration by the world through the use of wolves (false teachers, false prophets, false shepherds, and false messiahs) who lead Christians astray from Christ and entice them to sin.

Satan prefers this strategy because he knows that he cannot stop God from giving success to righteous men who are fighting against the forces of darkness. However, he also knows that God is holy and cannot tolerate sin. So, he tempts the church to sin, ruining the church's witness, causing them to blaspheme the name of Christ, and bringing God's chastisement on them. The best example of this is the story of Balaam (which is referenced numerous times in the Bible because of its importance), who tempted the Israelites to commit sexual sin, which became a stumbling block to them (Numbers 22-25, Deuteronomy 23:3-6, 2 Peter 2:15, Jude 11, and Revelation 2:14). This story has played out innumerable times throughout the history of Israel and the church and every time it does, Satan sees it as a victory (although he should not, since the effects are always temporary and God continues to accomplish His good and perfect plan despite the evil intentions of the enemy).

In Sheep's Clothing

The purpose of this book is to look at the growing influence of wolves who are pushing heretical Neo-Nazi false doctrines, but many wolves and many false teachings threaten the church right now. It is vitally important that Christians know how to recognize these wolves. In Matthew 7:13-23, Jesus said,

> Enter through the narrow gate; for the gate is wide and the way is broad that leads to destruction, and there are many who enter through it. For the gate is small and the way is narrow that leads to life, and there are few who find it. Beware of the false prophets, who come to you in sheep's clothing, but inwardly are ravenous wolves. You will know them by their fruits. Grapes are not gathered from thorn bushes nor figs from thistles, are they? So every good tree bears good fruit, but the bad tree bears bad fruit. A good tree cannot produce bad fruit, nor can a bad

tree produce good fruit. Every tree that does not bear good fruit is cut down and thrown into the fire. So then, you will know them by their fruits. Not everyone who says to Me, "Lord, Lord," will enter the kingdom of heaven, but he who does the will of My Father who is in heaven will enter. Many will say to Me on that day, "Lord, Lord, did we not prophesy in Your name, and in Your name cast out demons, and in Your name perform many miracles?" And then I will declare to them, "I never knew you; depart from me, you who practice lawlessness."

It is quite probable that many of today's "Christians" will stand before Christ on Judgment Day, unknown to Him, and will ask, "Lord, did we not fight 'trashworld' in Your name? Did we not raise big families? Were we not 'based' and right-wing? Since we were not gay, doesn't that make us good people? Didn't we oppose feminism and Zionism in Your name?" If you are an unrepentant worker of lawlessness who does not know Christ, none of these things will save you.

There are two critical lessons to learn from this passage. First, *many* people are on the broad path which leads to destruction and *many* people who claim to be Christians, "followers of God," pastors, prophets, influencers, podcasters, teachers, and even miracle workers are not real Christians. You cannot trust that someone is a real Christian or a follower of God just because they claim to be Christian or use Christian language. Even if they seem very spiritual, this is not evidence that they are the real deal. Truly, this is one of the most terrifying passages in the Bible. On the Day of Judgment, many Christians who struggle with discernment will be shocked to find out that Christ never knew many of their favorite "Christian" friends, pastors, teachers, podcasters, and theologians. They will discover that the only things these "Christians" actually cared about was money, fame, and, ultimately, sin.

Recognizing Wolves

Second, it is possible to recognize wolves by examining their fruits. All Christians should be discerning and should carefully examine the lives and teachings of other Christians who have influence in their lives. 1 John 4:1 says, "Beloved, do not believe every spirit, but test the spirits to see whether they are from God, because many false prophets have gone out into the world." And what is this "bad fruit" which indicates that someone is a wolf? It is a lifestyle of practicing lawlessness (Matthew 7:23), which can be seen in the wolf's words, deeds, or both.

1 John 3:4-8 states,

Everyone who practices sin also practices lawlessness; and sin is lawlessness. You know that He appeared in order to take away sins; and in Him there is no sin. No one who abides in Him sins; no one who sins has seen Him or knows Him. Little children, make sure no one deceives you; the one who practices righteousness is righteous, just as He is righteous; the one who practices sin is of the devil; for the devil has sinned from the beginning.

Clearly, it is possible for a Christian to sin (Romans 7:14-25). But if someone has a lifestyle which is characterized by unrepentant lawlessness or advocating for lawlessness, there is no reason to think such a person knows God; rather, there is every reason to believe that this person is of the devil.

The task of recognizing these wolves can be challenging for those who are not intimately familiar with their Bible. After all, wolves almost always claim to be Christians and are willing to chant slogans like "Christ is King." Wolves oftentimes are regular churchgoers, honor Christ with their lips and lead their congregations in worship songs and hymns (Isaiah 29:13 and Matthew 15:8), and are very knowledgeable about the Bible. Even Satan will quote Scripture out of context to tempt us, as evidenced by the story of Jesus in the wilderness, described in Matthew 4:1-11. Although these wolves teach and practice things which are contrary to the teachings of the Bible, their knowledge allows them to debate and humiliate real Christians who challenge them, but who are foolishly not very familiar with the Bible themselves.

It is common for wolves to be very clean, polite, friendly, charming, witty, and to have a disarming sense of humor. Additionally, many wolves dress very sharply and have excellent "physiognomy," possessing good looks, symmetrical faces, and neatly trimmed beards. Many of them are very intelligent and have a high IQ. A wolf may even be very emphatic about his belief that he is called by God to the ministry. Ironically, the more Biblically literate, "religious," and "called" a wolf is, the more dangerous he will be to others. As C.S. Lewis pointed out, "If the Divine call does not make us better, it will make us very much worse. Of all bad men religious bad men are the worst."[28]

To be safe from the destructive influence of wolves, Christians must stop judging others by their appearance. In John 7:24, Jesus warned, "Do not judge according to appearance, but judge with righteous judgment." We should imitate God, who said, "Do not look at his appearance or at the height of his stature, because I have rejected him; for God sees not as man sees, for man looks at the outward appearance, but the LORD looks at the heart," (1 Samuel 16:7). After all, Jesus himself did not have a desirable physical appearance during His earthly ministry, as it says in Isaiah 53:2-3:

> For He grew up before Him like a tender shoot, and like a root out of parched ground; He has no stately form or majesty that we should look upon Him, nor appearance that we should be attracted to Him. He was despised and forsaken of men, a man of sorrows and acquainted with grief; and like one from whom

---

[28] Lewis, C. (1958). *Reflections on the Psalms.* Pg. 36. William Collins, an imprint of HarperCollins Publishers.

men hide their face He was despised, and we did not esteem Him.

Conversely, Satan himself has a very attractive appearance and "disguises himself as an angel of light" (2 Corinthians 11:14).

Christians cannot rely on or even factor appearances into their discernment, because they are so often deceptive. In light of the Bible's teachings on this subject, statements like the following from Pastor Joel Webbon are very dangerous: "Our external appearance can often mirror the reality of our soul. So while physiognomy isn't perfect, there certainly is a place for it in the discerning Christian's arsenal."[29] Saying that "physiognomy isn't perfect" is a massive understatement, considering that Scripture says that the Lord of Lords and King of Kings Himself did not have an attractive appearance and was like a person who people hide their faces from, while Satan appears to be an angel of light. There is *no place* for judging by appearances in a discerning Christian's arsenal, when we are explicitly instructed not to judge by outward appearance and not to

---

[29] Webbon, J. (2025, February 11). *The stereotype of the arrogant jock contrasted to the humble nerd is overdone and generally not even true. Our external...* [Post]. X. https://x.com/rightresponsem/status/1889372662918521118

consider a man's physique. With teaching like this, it is no wonder that so many Christians are being led astray into destructive heresies like Neo-Nazism by good-looking, intelligent teachers.

Recognizing the Voice of Christ

To be able to discern wolves and the lawlessness which characterizes their lives and ministries, Christians must recognize the voice of Christ. In John 10:1-5, Jesus says,

> Truly, truly, I say to you, he who does not enter by the door into the fold of the sheep, but climbs up some other way, he is a thief and a robber. But he who enters by the door is a shepherd of the sheep. To him the doorkeeper opens, and the sheep hear his voice, and he calls his own sheep by name and leads them out. When he puts forth all his own, he goes ahead of them, and the sheep follow him because they know his voice. A stranger they simply will not follow, but will flee from him, because they do not know the voice of strangers.

And how can you know the voice of Christ? The answer is simple: Jesus is the Word of God (John 1:1) and the Bible is the Word of God, so you should carefully study every detail of the Bible from cover to cover. You could spend one hundred years studying the Word of God and you would not come close to learning everything there is to learn from it. But the more you study it, the better you will know His voice.

Why do so many Christians fail to study the Bible and fall into snares of wolves? In 2 Timothy 4:3-4, Paul warned that a time was coming when people,

> [...] will not endure sound doctrine; but wanting to have their ears tickled, they will accumulate for themselves teachers in accordance to their own desires, and will turn away their ears from the truth and will turn aside to myths.

Christians who become victims of wolves are those who care more about race, conspiracy theories about the Jews, and myths like Bigfoot, Atlantis, mermaids, and Mothman than they care about hearing the entirety of the Word of God being faithfully and truthfully exposited. These Christians will deliberately avoid large swaths of Scripture for their entire lives because many Bible passages make them deeply uncomfortable, but they will gladly listen to hours of podcasts that talk about things which tickle their ears (such as how the United States was actually fighting on the wrong side of World War II; conspiracies about how the Jews run the porn industry and the government; the virtue of having good physiognomy or high IQ; or why racism and sexism aren't actually sinful).

Those who only listen to such myths and things that tickle their ears are not being challenged to grow in the holiness of God; it is the equivalent of eating nothing but junk food. Not only will you not grow in godliness, but a diet only consisting of junk food will wreak havoc on your body. As your spiritual immune system is destroyed you will be sick all the time. Not only will you feel awful, but you will then spread these illnesses to others, making you a danger to be around.

A true man of God will not be content with the foolish teachings of wolves. Rather, he will seek instruction from the entire Word of God and will especially desire to study passages which he does not understand and which make him uncomfortable. He will allow the Word of God to have complete authority over his life and will change his beliefs to align with the Word, even if it means losing popularity with his friends, family, and followers. In 2 Timothy 3:16-17, Paul commented, "All Scripture is inspired by God and profitable for teaching, for reproof, for correction, for training in righteousness; so that the man of God may be adequate, equipped for every good work."

2 John 9-11 warns,

Anyone who goes too far and does not abide in the teaching of Christ, does not have God; the one who abides in the teaching, he has both the Father and the Son. If anyone comes to you and does not bring this teaching, do not receive him into your house, and do not give him a greeting; for the one who gives him a greeting participates in his evil deeds.

Many wolves and their followers start out teaching and learning the truth about Christ. But when they realize it is less uncomfortable and more enjoyable (and, for the wolf, profitable) to learn about and teach heresies, conspiracy theories, politics, myths, and other inflammatory things which are strange and perverse, they will happily abandon their regular study and exposition of the teachings of Christ and the Word of God in favor of topical teachings on these bizarre subjects. Occasionally, they will return to the truth to convince themselves and others that they are still Christians. But true love for Christ and His Word does not consistently abide in their lives anymore.

Why Wolues Are Pimping Out Christ's Bride to the Nazis

Why do wolves lead people astray? First and foremost, it is because they love darkness more than light (John 3:19). But in practical terms, it is because they love money and fame. They want people to be impressed with them, give them respect, and come to them for advice as "spiritual fathers," which is something they take great pride in. They want to be able to say "I'm one of the best we've got", like Pastor Joel Webbon has claimed.[30]

Also like Webbon, they want their names to be remembered by others. Webbon mocked Pastor Tobias Riemenschneider (who expressed serious concerns about the dark direction Webbon was moving in) by proclaiming, "This is why the young men will continue to come to me,

---

[30] Smothers, C. (2024, November 26). *The Apostle Paul: "I am the very least of all the saints" (Eph. 3:8). John the Baptist: "He must increase…* [Post]. X. https://x.com/colinsmo/status/1861466027445350431

and no one will remember your name."[31] They want to provide a comfortable (or, sometimes, extravagant) lifestyle for themselves and their families, without doing real work with their hands or having to be bossed around by someone (more than anything in the world, they loathe the idea of submitting to an employer), by making money from book deals, conferences, donations, online subscriptions, and speaking fees.

And for these petty, fleeting pleasures, wolves are willing to sell their souls; blaspheme and take the name of God of in vain; give Satan an opportunity to attack and weaken the church; and pimp out the Bride of Christ for money, turning her into a Hitler-worshipping, Jew-hating, Nazi whore.

However, the saints can praise God because, in the end, He will destroy these wolves, even if they escape judgment in their temporal lives. In 2 Peter 2:1-3 and 17-22, the Apostle warns,

> But false prophets also arose among the people, just as there will also be false teachers among you, who

---

[31] Right Response Ministries. (2024, October 2). *When A Member In Our Church Shared A Holocaust Meme* [Video]. YouTube. https://www.youtube.com/watch?v=pj7L7b66xLY&t=5063s

will secretly introduce destructive heresies, even denying the Master who bought them, bringing swift destruction upon themselves. Many will follow their sensuality, and because of them the way of the truth will be maligned; and in their greed they will exploit you with false words; their judgment from long ago is not idle, and their destruction is not asleep. [...]

These are springs without water and mists driven by a storm, for whom the black darkness has been reserved. For speaking out arrogant words of vanity they entice by fleshly desires, by sensuality, those who barely escape from the ones who live in error, promising them freedom while they themselves are slaves of corruption; for by what a man is overcome, by this he is enslaved. For if, after they have escaped the defilements of the world by the knowledge of the Lord and Savior Jesus Christ, they are again entangled in them and are overcome, the last state has become worse for them than the first. For it would be better for them not to have known the way of righteousness, than having known it, to turn away from the holy commandment handed on to them. It has happened to them according to the true proverb, "A dog returns to its own vomit," and, "A sow, after washing, returns to wallowing in the mire." Every bit of this frightful warning applies to the wolves who push Nazi doctrines on the church.

The Swastika in the Sanctuary

Chapter II: Nazism

When I started to witness the rise and rapid proliferation of Nazi propaganda on social media (particularly X) in 2024, mostly among right-wing Reformed or Catholic Christian Nationalists, I was very skeptical as to their authenticity. It seemed absurd that hundreds of thousands, if not millions, of "Christians" would be sharing and liking filthy, disgusting posts and saying that "Hitler was right about the Jews," "we owe Hitler an apology," and, even, "it's cool to be a Nazi." After all, it was an election year, and conspiracy theorists were fond of claiming that Biden's federal law enforcement agencies were conducting a psyop to make Trump supporters look like Nazis. There was not a single piece of evidence to support this claim and good reasons to believe it wasn't true, but this propaganda was repeated so much and so confidently by pundits that it was almost impossible to not consider it a possibility.

Even though the overwhelming mood and consensus on social media and X was that Donald Trump was going to win the election, I also was suspicious that this consensus was manufactured, fake, or otherwise not representative of the true sentiments of the American people. However, Donald Trump handily won the election, proving that the mood on X was *accurate*, to my great surprise. If X really did accurately represent the sentiments of Americans, what does this say about the massively growing Neo-Nazi movement which is manifest on the platform? It suggests the Nazi propaganda accounts and followers are not entirely "bots" and this is not a manufactured consensus, but a real cancer that is growing.

Even after Donald Trump was elected and took control of the federal agencies, the Nazi propaganda only got *worse* on social media, making it even less likely that there was ever any federal involvement in propagating this phenomenon to make Republicans look bad. Additionally, an increasing number of these larger anonymous accounts are getting "doxxed", a term that refers to identifying the personal information of a public figure, often revealing the name of an anonymous account. When this happens, they are commonly discovered to be pastors of Reformed churches, worship leaders, small business owners, and very normal people who could be your coworkers, friends, or family members. Most of those who are doxxed are young White men, although some are middle-aged.

I have never seen a report that any of these accounts have been doxxed and discovered to be bots or feds. Logically, it is likely that *some* of these anonymous accounts are bots or nefarious state actors, but it has been proven with hard evidence that *many* are not. Furthermore, as we have seen and will continue to see, there are many pastors, teachers, and other influencers who are openly pushing Nazi doctrines with their real names and who have massive support from real followers who show up at their conferences, purchase their books, and subscribe to their content. In retrospect, it is apparent that the conservative pundits who were making this claim without any evidence—that *all* of the rising Nazism on the Right could be attributed to bots or feds—were trying to explain away the dark element which was gaining traction on their team. It was easier and more comfortable to blame this growing problem on these forces rather than deal with the fact that a significant portion of the grassroots base on the Right were true, unapologetic, Hitler-loving, Jew-hating, swastika-brandishing Nazis.

Furthermore, Christian pastors, teachers, and church members are increasingly reporting that young men in their churches or social circles are being radicalized by Nazi-sympathizing "Christian" podcasters or influencers. I have personally observed this myself. Not only is it disturbing to watch this radicalization of young men in our church occur, but it is also horrifying to see conservative Christians (who would not describe themselves as Nazis) come to the defense of those who do describe themselves as Nazis.

This Neo-Nazi nonsense did not stop after the 2024 election. Instead, right-wing influencers who claim to be Christians continue to say more and more vile and unhinged things. For instance, Corey Mahler, responding to a post commemorating the 80th anniversary of Nazi Propaganda Minister Joseph Goebels murdering his children and committing suicide because he did not want to live in a world without Hitler, stated, "This was his Christian duty under those circumstances. If you do not understand this fact, then you are no man and should remain silent."[32]

---

[32] Mahler, C. (2025, May 1). *This was his Christian duty under those circumstances. If you do not understand this fact, then you are no man…* [Post]. X. https://x.com/CoreyJMahler/status/1918006063456240047

In response to a minister who critiqued Mahler's vile statement, Wesley Todd, co-host of Pastor Joel Webbon's Right Response Ministries podcast, commented, "It's a tragic situation but I would do the same if my family was going to brutalized [sic] by the red army."[33] When Todd was confronted that he was using the same logic as those who advocate for abortion based on future suffering, he doubled down by saying, "There's a difference between hypothetical suffering and imminent, guaranteed brutality [and] death."[34] So to avoid the Red Army murdering the Goebbels children (which was not guaranteed; Joseph Goebbels refused an opportunity to escape with his family and surrender to the Americans), was Joseph Goebbels justified in murdering them himself? Until recently, this type of logic was used primarily by abortion supporters who justify abortion because of the imminent threat of poverty, abuse, or health problems to the child. Now it is also used by some right-wing influencers who call themselves Christians.

---

[33] Todd, W. (2025, May 1). *It's a tragic situation but I would do the same if my family was going to brutalized by the red...* [Post]. X. https://x.com/Wesley_Todd_/status/1918043047390032378

[34] Todd, W. (2025, May 1). There's a difference between hypothetical suffering and imminent, guaranteed brutality + death. [Post]. X. https://x.com/Wesley_Todd_/status/1918159826812621045

Another example of the absurd propaganda that continues to be pushed is the total demonization of Winston Churchill and the humanization or glorification of Adolf Hitler. For instance, in a February 2025 podcast, Joel Webbon described Churchill as a "maniac" and a "warmonger" "who refused peace" and said,

> Churchill made it [World War II] the world's problem. He did. He forced, he was like, everyone is going to deal with this... Great Britain, you know, the empire for which the sun never sets, well the sun kind of was setting on Great Britain. And they didn't really like it and they needed to, they weren't just caring about virtue and "oh the principles!" There was some of that. But there was also a sense of, "No... we're the superpower of Europe. We're Great Britain. Germany can't supersede us." And so this thing became a global affair and here's the deal, everybody lost.[35]

Compare this with Webbon's teachings on Hitler in June 2025:

---

[35] Right Response Ministries. (2025, February 19). *Yes, the Gospel Changes Genetics* [Video]. YouTube. https://www.youtube.com/live/X6DamHcx8t8

Why can't we have nice things in the West like tradition and nationalism and a love for our people? [...] Why can't we have America First? Why can't we have these kinds of things? And of course the answer is because of the Austrian painter with a funny mustache. [...] Why can't we have those basic thoughts and beliefs? Because of an Austrian painter who might, depending on your World War II history, might have been a little overly zealous. […]

I'm not wanting to lionize Hitler or have some kind of Third Reich renaissance but I am very hopeful that we could get over Hitler; not obsess about him, but get over Hitler to where we're able to humanize him. Continue to name whatever was truly wicked but also be able to see, okay, there's probably some reasons why people are looking to Weimar Germany and seeing the parallels and these kinds of things. […]

Why can we not have nice things in the west? Because of in large part the post-war consensus and the 'never again' mentality and people attributing certain atrocities of authoritarian figures to the emphasis towards tradition, nationalism, patriarchy.[36]

Historical records from World War II clearly show that it was Hitler, not Churchill, who was a "maniac" and "warmonger" "who refused peace," by invading multiple innocent countries and violating numerous peace agreements, including the Treaty of Versailles, the Locarno Pact, the Munich Agreement, the German-Polish Non-Agression Pact, and the German-Soviet Non-Agression Pact. Webbon's comments here display such a distortion of history they call into question how it is possible in this age of information to have such stunning ignorance. Referring to Hitler as someone who "might have been a little overly zealous" is an incredible understatement for someone who murdered millions of Jews and martyred many faithful Christians, including Hans and Sophie Scholl, Catholic students in Germany who were beheaded for the crime of distributing pamphlets decrying the atrocities committed by the Nazi regime.

---

[36] Mantyla, K. (2025, June 9). Joel Webbon Hopes The World Will Soon Learn To 'Humanize' Hitler. People for the American Way. https://www.peoplefor.org/rightwingwatch/joel-webbon-hopes-world-will-soon-learn-humanize-hitler

Attributing nothing but evil to those who fought for good, like Churchill, and handling wicked mass-murderers and Christian-killers, like Hitler, with kid gloves flies in the face of Isaiah 5:20, which warns, "Woe to those who call evil good, and good evil; who substitute darkness for light and light for darkness; who substitute bitter for sweet and sweet for bitter!"

Also in June 2025, Corey Mahler stated, "If you still think that Hitler overreacted, then you deserve to spend your last days a hated and hunted minority in the smoldering ruins of the civilization your forefathers failed to preserve."[37] The same day, he said, "Every Jew Hitler killed (certainly far fewer than six million) is in Hell. Adolf Hitler is in Paradise. In the end analysis, who really won?"[38] In March 2025, he commented, "Adolf Hitler is in Paradise; Dietrich Bonhoeffer [a Christian who attempted to assassinate Hitler] is in Hell. Christians may praise only one of these men."[39] In

---

[37] Mahler, C. (2025, June 6). *If you still think that Hitler overreacted, then you deserve to spend your last days a hated and hunted minority…* [Post]. X. https://x.com/CoreyJMahler/status/1931085895727292513

[38] Mahler, C. (2025, June 6). *Every Jew Hitler killed (certainly far fewer than six million) is in Hell. Adolf Hitler is in Paradise. In the…* [Post]. X. https://x.com/CoreyJMahler/status/1931125166253244611

[39] Mahler, C. (2025, March 17). *Adolf Hitler is in Paradise; Dietrich Bonhoeffer is in Hell. Christians may praise only one of these men.* [Post]. X. https://x.com/CoreyJMahler/status/1901782761737683025

April 2025, Mahler taught, "There will be men in Hell whose damning sin was elevating hatred of Hitler and 'Nazis' above love of God."[40] In March 2025, Mahler stated, "There isn't a single, honest man alive who would rather live in the modern United States than in Hitler's Germany. Liberty is nothing in the face of things that truly matter — duty is everything."[41] Additionally, in December 2024, Mahler pronounced, "Adolf Hitler's opposition to the Jews is proof of his Christian faith."[42]

As anyone who is active on X can testify, the propagation of Nazi doctrines did not stop after the 2024 election; rather, it has exploded in popularity. Even so, the current Nazi-sympathizing movement, which is taking off with young male Christians in the Western world, is still in its fledgling state. Like the 1920's German National Socialist movement, it is possible that this movement could spawn a charismatic leader and become a more extreme problem for

---

[40] Mahler, C. (2025, April 5). *There will be men in Hell whose damning sin was elevating hatred of Hitler and 'Nazis' above love of God.* [Post]. X. https://x.com/CoreyJMahler/status/1908685380817211564

[41] Mahler, C. (2025, March 1). *There isn't a single, honest man alive who would rather live in the modern United States than in Hitler's Germany.* [Post]. X. https://x.com/CoreyJMahler/status/1896014510026342776

[42] Mahler, C. (2024, December 9). *Adolf Hitler's opposition to the Jews is proof of his Christian faith.* https://x.com/CoreyJMahler/status/1866232348183756970

the nations of the West soon. If this happens, it could take anywhere from a few years to a few decades for the movement to reach maturity and begin its next murderous rampage. Hopefully, however, God will destroy this dark revival in its infancy and it will die the same death that thousands of other heresies throughout history have suffered.

Is Nazism Compatible With Christianity?

When looking at this movement, it is crucial to be able to answer the following question: is it actually wrong for someone to be a Nazi or a Nazi-sympathizer? Variations of this question are being asked by those who seek to defend their right-wing "brothers" who have been snared by Nazi false doctrines. According to the Bible, the answer is a very strong "yes." It is wrong for someone to take counsel from the wicked (which certainly includes living and dead proponents of Nazi ideology); it is wrong for someone to enter the path of the wicked and follow in their steps; it is wrong to keep company with the wicked because this will inevitably affect your character; and it is wrong to be envious of the wicked or even to desire to be in their presence.

Psalm 1:1-2 and 6 states,

How blessed is the man who does not walk in the counsel of the wicked, nor stand in the path of sinners, nor sit in the seat of scoffers! But his delight is in the law of the LORD, and in His law he meditates day and night. [...] For the LORD knows the way of the righteous, but the way of the wicked will perish.

Proverbs 4:14-17 warns against and perfectly describes the wicked, violent company of Nazis:

Do not enter the path of the wicked and do not proceed in the way of evil men. Avoid it, do not pass by it; turn away from it and pass on. For they cannot sleep unless they do evil; and they are robbed of sleep unless they make someone stumble. For they eat the bread of wickedness and drink the wine of violence.

1 Corinthians 15:33 says, "Do not be deceived: 'Bad company corrupts good morals.'" 1 Corinthians 5:9-13 forbids Christians from associating with anyone who claims to be a Christian but lives a life of gross sin. Ephesians 5:11 states, "Do not participate in the unfruitful deeds of darkness, but instead even expose them." Additionally, Proverbs

24:1-2 comments, "Do not be envious of evil men, nor desire to be with them; for their minds devise violence, and their lips talk of trouble."

"Well, sure," one might argue, "I guess I can agree that it is wrong for Christians to take the company and counsel of the wicked. But were the Nazis actually that evil? And is it really that bad for someone to associate with something that is ultimately just a political movement from the 20th century?"

Many books have been written on the evils which have been perpetrated and advocated for by the National Socialist German Workers' (Nazi) Party since its inception. Since many conservative Christians who defend Nazi-sympathizers seem to have forgotten these things, I will summarize a few of the key problems with Nazism which highlight why the Nazis of the past and present can undeniably be described as the "wicked."

The Degeneracy of the Nazis

First, Nazism is explicitly anti-Christian and opposed to the church, according to high-ranking Nazis themselves. Martin Bormann, who was one of the closest men to Hitler (as his secretary and as the head of the Nazi Party Chancellery), publicly said the following in 1941: "National Socialism and Christianity are irreconcilable."[43]

Additionally, in *The Nazi Primer: Official Handbook for Schooling of the Hitler Youth,* Nazi young people were taught that National Socialism opposed the "Christian Church" because of its beliefs on race:

> Even today the racial ideas of National Socialism have implacable opponents. Free Masons, Marxists, and the Christian Church join hands in brotherly accord on this point. The worldview order of Free Masons conceals its Jewish plans for ruling the world behind the catchword "Mankind" or "Humanity." Masonry can take as much credit for its effort to bring Jews and Turks into the fold as does Christianity itself. Marxism has the same goal as Free Masonry. In this case, to disguise its real intentions the slogan "Equality, Liberty and Fraternity" is preached. Under Jewish leadership Marxism intends to bring together everyone "who bears the face of man." The Christians, above all the Roman Church,

---

[43] Shirer, W. (1960). *The Rise and Fall of the Third Reich.* Pg. 240. Simon & Schuster.

reject the race idea with the citation "before God all men are equal." All who have the Christian belief, whether Jews, bush niggers, or whites, are dearer to them and more worthwhile than a German who does not confess Christianity. The one binding bond, above and beyond all restrictions, is the Belief which alone brings salvation."[44]

Coincidentally, a number of Nazi-sympathizing wolves have recently started to make the same claims: that American Christians are obligated to non-Christian Americans more than Christians from other nations, that the Jews are behind Communism, and that the church is a stumbling block to their ambitions. Did they knowingly steal these ideas verbatim from the Nazis? That certainly seems possible for many of these wolves. Or, for other false teachers, it could be that they have been unknowingly led astray by the same being, Satan, who is lazily recycling his old deceptions and talking points.

---

[44] Brennecke, F. (1938). *The Nazi Primer: Official Handbook for Schooling of the Hitler Youth.* Pp. 9-10. Harper & Brothers Publishers. (H. Childs & W. Dodd trans.). https://archive.org/details/the-nazi-primer/mode/2up (Original work published 1937).

Not only is Nazism anti-Christian, but it is one of the most blasphemous and idolatrous movements which has ever existed in human history. Anyone familiar with history and with present-day Neo-Nazis knows that the movement reveres Adolf Hitler as a god and makes preservation of race the most important thing in life, a true idol that takes precedence over all else. The following is an example of this blasphemy, which can be found in some of the thirty articles of the "National Reich Church" plan, which was put together by the outspoken pagan Alfred Rosenberg, a Nazi theorist and head of the Office of Foreign Affairs:

> The National Reich Church of Germany categorically claims the exclusive right and the exclusive power to control all churches within the borders of the Reich: it declares these to be national churches of the German Reich. [...] The National Church is determined to exterminate irrevocably [...] the strange and foreign Chrisitan faiths imported into Germany in the ill-omened year 800. [...] The National Church has no scribes, pastors, chaplains or priests, but National Reich orators are to speak in them. [...] The National Church demands immediate

cessation of the publishing and dissemination of the Bible in Germany. […] The National Church declares that to it, and therefore to the German nation, it has been decided that the Fuehrer's *Mein Kampf* is the greatest of all documents. It […] not only contains the greatest but it embodies the purest and truest of ethics for the present and future life of our nation. […] The National Church will clear away from its altars all crucifixes, Bibles and pictures of saints. On the altars there must be nothing but *Mein Kampf* (to the German nation and therefore to God the most sacred book) and to the left of the altar a sword. […] On the day of its foundation, the Christian Cross must be removed from all churches, cathedrals and chapels […] and it must be superseded by the only unconquerable symbol, the swastika."[45]

A similar example of modern-day blasphemy can be seen in the following statement from Corey Mahler: "One of the greatest uses of the hooked cross (the 'swastika') is

---

[45] Shirer, W. (1960). *The Rise and Fall of the Third Reich*. Pg. 240. Simon & Schuster.

detecting enemies by watching who recoils from it—like a vampire from a cross."[46]

Additionally, Nazism is responsible for the murder of innocents. At least six million Jews were primarily shot or gassed to death by the Nazis during the Holocaust. To this day, many Neo-Nazis and Nazi-sympathizers argue that the Jews deserved this punishment. Some will claim they do not believe the Holocaust happened, while also claiming, "the Jews deserved it," without having the self-awareness to realize that they contradicted themselves.

Not only did their hatred of the Jewish race drive the Nazis to murder innocent Jewish men, women, children, and entire families and communities, they did the same to other racial and ethnic groups. For example, after the previously mentioned Martin Bormann noticed how many children Slavic peoples had in Nazi-occupied Ukraine, he said in 1942, "In view of the large families of the native population, it could only suit us if girls and women there had as many abortions as possible."[47]

---

[46] Mahler, C. (2025, February 20). *One of the greatest uses of the hooked cross (the 'swastika') is detecting enemies by watching who recoils from it...* [Post]. X. https://x.com/CoreyJMahler/status/1892693940953927773
[47] Perry, M. (n.d.). As Many Abortions as Possible. Eternal World Television Network.

Shortly after making this observation, an order was issued which included the following directives, as Bormann desired:

> When girls and women in the Occupied Territories of the East have abortions, we can only be in favor of it; in any case we should not oppose it. The Führer believes that we should authorize the development of a thriving trade in contraceptives. We are not interested in seeing the non-German population multiply.[48]

This was not the first time the Nazis had done something like this. In Nazi occupied Poland in 1939, for instance, the Reich Commission for Strengthening of Germandom issued the following directive for Poland:

> All measures which have the tendency to limit the births are to be tolerated or to be supported. Abortion in the remaining area [of Poland] must be declared free from punishment. The means for abortion and contraceptive means may be offered publicly without police restriction. Homosexuality is always to be

---

https://www.ewtn.com/catholicism/library/as-many-abortions-as-possible-12118
[48] Ibid.

declared legal. The institutions and persons involved professionally in abortion practices are not to be interfered with by police.[49]

Likewise, in 1942, Ehrard Wetzel, who worked for the Nazi's Office of Racial Policy, issued the following directive regarding the Russian people:

> Every propaganda means, especially the press, radio, and movies, as well as pamphlets, booklets, and lectures, must be used to instill in the Russian population the idea that it is harmful to have several children. We must emphasize the expenses that children cause, the good things that people could have had with the money spent on them. We could also hint at the dangerous effect of child-bearing on a woman's health. Paralleling such propaganda, a large-scale campaign would be launched in favor of contraceptive devices. A contraceptive industry must be established. Neither the circulation and sale of contraceptives nor abortions must be prosecuted. It will even be necessary to open special institutions for abortion, and to train midwives and nurses for this

---

[49] Ibid.

purpose. The population will practice abortion all the more willingly if these institutions are competently operated. The doctors must be able to help [with]out there being any question of this being a breach of their professional ethics. Voluntary sterilization must also be recommended by propaganda.[50]

This same type of reasoning is prevalent today, with an increasing number of far right-wing commentators arguing that abortion is fine as long as it is done by non-Whites or liberals. For instance, Tim Pool, a conservative influencer with millions of followers, has stated:

> Everyday the cultural divide gets worse… If we want to end the culture war we have to compromise on abortion and gender affirming surgeries… as the leftists sterilize and 'excise' their children from society the course will begin to correct itself.[51]

Further, Pool commented, "Gender affirmation and abortion is a win win for the US… Liberals get to live their

---

[50] Ibid.
[51] Pool, T. (2023, May 17). *everyday the cultural divide gets worse If we want to end the culture war we have to compromise on abortion…* [Post]. X. https://x.com/Timcast/status/1658851534417846275

best lives... And conservatives get the future."[52] On top of this, Pool added, "Im [sic] torn on the issue of abortion... on the one hand its killing a baby... on the other its a liberals [sic] baby."[53]

The Nazis not only murdered innocents and promoted abortion, but they also encouraged a litany of vices in nations that they desired to destroy. For instance, the Nazis flooded Poland with pornography to weaken its people, as the historian Ihor Kamenetsky noted,

> The German Propaganda Office [...] was supposed to organize or sponsor Polish burlesque shows and publish cheap literature, strongly erotic in nature. . . . to keep the masses on a low level and to divert their interest from political aspirations. These projects for degeneration and moral debasement were actually realized in the larger Polish cities.[54]

---

[52] Pool, T. (2023, May 22). *gender affirmation and abortion is a win win for the US Liberals get to live their best lives And conservatives...* [Post]. X. https://x.com/Timcast/status/1660698392412995608

[53] Pool, T. (2024, February 29). *im torn on the issue of abortion on the one hand its killing a baby on the other its a...* [Post]. X. https://x.com/Timcast/status/1763221019299316062

[54] Perry, M. (n.d.). As Many Abortions as Possible. Eternal World Television Network. https://www.ewtn.com/catholicism/library/as-many-abortions-as-possible-12118

To this day, Neo-Nazis and Nazi sympathizers ironically claim that Jews are responsible for flooding the internet with pornography to destroy their enemies, unaware or unwilling to admit that it was the Nazis who actually did this.

Drug usage was also rampant in Nazi Germany, especially Pervitin, a potent methamphetamine drug. The Nazis gave copious amounts of this drug to German soldiers during World War II. When they were high on this drug, Nazis had sharp focus and alertness, high morale, reduced fear and inhibition, excellent endurance, and suppressed anxiety. The drug allowed Nazis to fight at peak performance without eating or sleeping for days. This has caused some historians, like Norman Ohler (who wrote the fascinating book *Blitzed: Drugs in the Third Reich*), to assert that one of the primary reasons the Nazis experienced such success at the beginning of World War II during the Blitzkrieg was due to their usage of methamphetamine. Ironically, Nazi leadership bought their own propaganda and started to believe that the excellent performance of their troops was actually due to them being "Aryan super soldiers," instead of remembering that their success was primarily due to drug usage. This feeling of invincibility led Nazi High Command to make horrible strategic blunders, like Operation Barbarossa, later in the war.

When it comes to the sin of hypocrisy, Nazism is filled with inconsistency on the topic of homosexuality. Despite some Nazis claiming that Nazism was opposed to homosexuality, it is well documented that homosexuality was rampant from the very founding of the Nazi party with many of its early members[55] and that Hitler was fine with this. As war correspondent William Shirer reported, "Murderers, pimps, homosexual perverts, drug addicts or just plain rowdies were all the same to [Hitler] if they served his purposes."[56] Not only were many of the early rank and file Nazis homosexuals, but there were also some notorious homosexuals in leadership positions close to Hitler.[57]

Homosexuality continued to play an important role in Nazism through the rest of the years of the Third Reich. For instance, due to the number of male Nazi guards who were witnessed raping male prisoners in concentration camps, it is estimated that 20% of the Nazi soldiers who were guarding

---

[55] Shirer, W. (1960). *The Rise and Fall of the Third Reich.* Pg. 38. Simon & Schuster.
[56] Ibid, pg. 50.
[57] Ibid, pg. 120.

Jews were homosexual[58] or bisexual. The elite Nazi SS soldiers, in particular, were males who were known for horrifically sexually abusing their male victims before murdering them.[59]

Additionally, since the end of World War II, widespread homosexuality has been practiced in the Neo-Nazi movement in America. George Lincoln Rockwell's American Nazi Party, for instance, was documented to be significantly composed of homosexual members.[60] Likewise, the President of the National Socialist Party of America, Frank Collin, who gained international media attention in 1977 when he led a Neo-Nazi march in Chicago, was convicted and sentenced to prison for seven years for molesting boys who were between the ages of ten and fourteen.[61] For more reading on this fascinating subject, I highly recommend Lively and Abrams' *The Pink Swastika*. This book documents unbridled homosexuality among rank and file and high-ranking Nazis of yesterday and today.

---

[58] Lively, S. and Abrams, K. (2002). *The Pink Swastika: Homosexuality in the Nazi Party*. Pg. 233. Veritas Aeterna Press.
[59] Ibid, pp. 240-241.
[60] Ibid, pp. 277-279.
[61] Ibid, pp. 279-280.

Since Nazis frequently claim that they are opposed to homosexuality, why is it so widespread among Nazis? The reason for this is actually fairly simple. Nazism glorifies men and masculinity to a level that is borderline or outright idolatrous, while showing disgust for women. Nazis believed (and still believe) that the only place for women "was in the kitchen and their chief role in life [was] to beget children for German warriors."[62] Nazis believe that women are weak, intellectually inferior to men, easily deceived, and foolish; essentially, they see women as loathsome children who must be subjugated by men. It is common for modern wolves who knowingly or unknowingly push Nazi doctrines to say things like "women should be seen, not heard," or "I don't want to see women in public at all."

On the other hand, these men find masculinity to be extremely attractive. They idolize a well-sculpted male body and constantly talk about the importance of working out (ostensibly this is because they care about health and fitness; in truth, however, it is because muscular male bodies turn them "on"). They fetishize the "physiognomy" of men, finding attraction in the symmetry of a man's face and the

---

[62] Shirer, W. (1960). *The Rise and Fall of the Third Reich*. Pg. 100. Simon & Schuster.

neatness in which his beard is kept. They rate pictures of men's faces side by side based on their physiognomy. If a man has unattractive physiognomy, he is not to be trusted; but if he has attractive physiognomy, he is probably a cool guy and a good man who is part of your team.

Nazis and Nazi-sympathizers who are homosexuals or who have homosexual desires will rarely admit to this. Instead, they try to keep this secret from the public, in part by labeling all of their enemies as "gay" even when they are not gay, a textbook example of projection. Even if their attractions are never fully exposed to the public, many hints of their secret desire will slip out. Any movement that simultaneously glorifies men and masculinity, fetishizes male bodies and physiognomy, and finds women to be repulsive is guaranteed to attract homosexuals and to turn many of its members gay, despite claiming to be opposed to homosexuality, making the movement massively hypocritical.

While Nazis and those who hold to Neo-Nazi false doctrines tend to keep quiet on their hidden homosexuality, some are known for advocating publicly for all manner of sick perversions. Nick Fuentes, for instance, who once proclaimed, "I love Hitler,"[63] stated the following on his podcast:

No, bitch. I wanna drink it straight from the tap. I wanna drink it raw. I don't wanna wait a moment. Right when the milk is good, I wanna start drinking the milk. Same thing goes with women. I don't wanna turn thirty and find some twenty-year-old, twenty-nine-year-old woman that I have something in common with and it's like, "Hey! Properly aged like wine!" Women don't age like wine; they age like milk. They don't age like wine. That's not how their hormones work. That's not how they work…

Yeah, I gotta find my sixteen-year-old wife. Probably when I turn thirty or something. Because here's the thing, I don't wanna be like, let's say I get married to an eighteen-year-old now. Six year age difference. When I turn forty she's gonna be thirty-four. Eww. But if I'm thirty and she's sixteen, fourteen year age difference, when I'm fifty, she'll be thirty-six. When I'm forty, she'll be twenty-six. Now

---

[63] Anti-Defamation League (2023, March 7). Fuentes Delivers Antisemitic, "Christian Nationalist" Rant to Fellow White Supremacists. https://www.adl.org/resources/article/fuentes-delivers-antisemitic-christian-nationalist-rant-fellow-white-supremacists

we're talking here. Now we're cooking with gas. Now you can see an alternative vision for how things could be…

I wanna sixteen-year-old who is untouched, pristine. Untouched, uncorrupted, innocent. That's what we all want. And all sixteen-year-olds want a [sic] older guy who's like capable and strong and everything to sweep them off their feet. That's what everybody wants. That's what everybody wants.[64]

Also in 2023, Fuentes advocated for abolishing the age of consent on his show:

I think the age of consent should be lower; I don't even really believe in the concept. You wanna know why? Because marriage is consent. You wanna know what's wrong with sex? Being married means you consent to sex all the time. There's no such thing as marital rape. Because, when you marry a person, you have a marital obligation to give your spouse sex whenever they want it! It's literally Catholic doctrine so…

---

[64] Right Wing Watch. (2023, May 17). *Misogynistic Christian fascist incel Nick Fuentes says that once he turns 30, he'll probably find himself a 16-year-old…* [Video]. X. https://x.com/RightWingWatch/status/1658865192128634882

Age of consent? What is this? What is this? Christians have no use for such things. Christians have no use for such a concept. You get married. A Christian doesn't have sex with anybody. A Christian has sex with their spouse within marriage. And nobody's getting married at a prepubescent age. People get married when they're at a reproductive age, when they're adolescents. And so then, you know, I'm just redefining it.[65]

Furthermore, Fuentes made the following very concerning remarks on his show:

When the Holy Spirit selected Mary, did the Holy Spirit go, "Let's look for a mature woman that I have something in common with?" Did a person of the Trinity go around and say, "Hmm… I need to find one of those mature women that is smart and has common interests and things in common with me"? Or did the Holy Spirit go and say, "I need a…" How old was the virgin Mary? I think she was like… well

---

[65] Popcorn. (2023, August 3). *Nicholas J. Fuentes and Andrew Anglin both believe that there is no such thing as of the "Age of Consent"…* [Video]. X. https://x.com/Popcorn1483/status/1687323263507333120

she wasn't eighteen, I'll say that much. Certainly wasn't eighteen.

[...] You know what I expect? A fertile womb. A fertile womb and a sort of innocent childlike spirit.

[...] Fuck you! I'm out here free-thinking, okay? And if I've got weird sexual interests and if I'm talking... if I'm dropping these redpills on you, you're going to shut up... "Stop dude! Stop!" Why? Am, am I scaring the hoes? Good. Fuck them hoes, okay?

[...] Okay, you wanna go to the correct opinion show, go watch TV. And you can watch all the correct opinions-havers tell you about how they want same-aged wives and they wanna talk about their interests and they wanna do normal, not-weird things, okay?

[...] Plenty of thirty-year-old fish in the sea for you guys, okay? Because I'm in the shallow end of the pool. Because I'm in the shallow end of the pool! Lookin' for them hoes that can't swim![66]

Additionally, Fuentes stated,

---

[66] Ibid.

As long as they are soldiers, look, I don't care how gay they are. As long as they're my loyal cult members that give me money and doxx hillbillies when I give the command.[67]

The optimist may wish to claim that Fuentes holds a niche view, not held by others. However, in June 2025, Joel Webbon did a podcast entitled, "Nick Fuentes Is Right, And We're Tired Of Pretending He's Not."[68] In an August 2025 podcast entitled, "The Power of Propaganda," Webbon said that "it would be great to see him [Nick] on the show [Webbon's podcast]." Webbon added, "If he's allowed to speak, he's going to win. [...] He's winning. And you may just not have admitted yet." Referring to Fuentes, later in the same show Webbon also stated, "The Overton window is moving right. Things that sounded crazy five years ago sound a lot less crazy today..." Later, Webbon said,

There are millions of young men who are following him [Fuentes]. And you wanna win the culture? Win the hearts of the young men, and he has. He has young men that he has won. [...] He does have power

---

[67] Ibid.

[68] Webbon, J. (2025, June 23). *Nick Fuentes Is Right, And We're Tired Of Pretending He's Not.* [Broadcast]. X. https://x.com/i/broadcasts/1yoJMozPaEDKQ

and influence with young men. And all these young men, you can sit there and say, "Well these young men live in their mother's basement." Well, number one, I don't think that's entirely true. For those that it is true, here's the thing about young men: eventually, they grow up. So these young men may not seem powerful now; right now it may just be their anon accounts and sheer numbers, just volume, loud on social media. [...] He's [Fuentes] got fifty years of potential relevancy and all of his following... they've got fifty years! Some of these guys will be CEO's. Some of these guys will be politicians. Some of them already are. [...] You're going to have to engage with Nick in terms of sheer influence, position, and relevance. [69]

In regards to this final point—that Fuentes is currently winning the hearts and minds of millions of young men who will become very powerful someday—Webbon is likely correct. But, this is nothing to celebrate, as these

---

[69] Right Response Ministries. (2025, August 1). *The Power of Propaganda* [Video]. YouTube. https://www.youtube.com/live/1FPBZ0NWHB0

young men are being seduced by Fuentes' degenerate, perverted influence.

No Christian should ever partner with a force for evil like Fuentes, who is corrupting the souls of young men. Instead, we have an incredible responsibility to fight this evil and expose the darkness, to help save the souls of those who are being led astray. Pastors in particular, who are responsible for guarding the souls of their flocks from wolves should be concerned about this. If a pastor does not care about this, or worse, partners with a wolf as he is devouring the flock, it is probably because the pastor is a wolf too.

In addition to what has been mentioned so far, Nazism has numerous other evils intrinsic to the movement and its ideology which I do not have space to elaborate on, but are well documented and can be easily researched. Some of these include: sorcery; pantheism and nature worship (on this topic, see Richard Weikart's fascinating book, *Hitler's Religion: The Twisted Beliefs that Drove the Third Reich*); astrology; paganism; Hitler-worship and idolatry; the telling and propagation of lies; totalitarianism, which is idolatry of the state; Marcionism (a heresy which teaches the Old

Testament is uninspired and the God of the Old Testament and the Jews is actually Satan); compelling unwilling innocents to undergo dangerous medical experimentation and forced vaccination; outlawing homeschooling and religious private schools; the persecution of Christians and the closure of churches which taught doctrines contrary to Nazism; the martyrdom of Christians who were acting in obedience to the Christian faith (like Franz Jägerstätter, an Austrian husband, father, and Catholic who was beheaded for refusing to swear an oath of obedience to Hitler); denying the right to keep and bear arms to civilians who were not members of the Nazi Party and to undesirable racial groups; encouraging and coercing young teenage girls to bear children out of wedlock for the Reich as a part of the Lebensborn Program; prostitution; eugenics; plans to legalize polygamy after World War II; and cowardice and suicide, as exemplified by the movement's failed, yet deified hero, Adolf Hitler.

Disguised as a Third Reich of Light

With all that being said, Nazis and Neo-Nazis certainly qualify as being among "the wicked" who Christians are forbidden from sympathizing with, associating with, being led by, or taking counsel from. But we have all heard the objection: Hitler did some good things, like restoring the German economy, bringing national pride and patriotism back to the people, and burning down transgender clinics. Is it wrong to sympathize with the good things the Nazis did?

The term "Nazi-sympathizer" is not used to describe someone who acknowledges that the Nazis did a *few* good things or that Neo-Nazis currently support a *few* good things. Many Neo-Nazis, for instance, encourage physical exercise and becoming healthy, something which almost everyone would agree is a good thing for people to do. Rather, it is used to describe someone who *generally* sympathizes with all that the Nazis are, all that they have done, and all that they stand for.

There is nothing wrong with acknowledging that an evil person or group of people did something right. For instance, it is widely believed (although it may be a myth) that Mussolini made the trains in Italy run on time. Just because Mussolini made the trains run on time does not mean that it is evil for trains to run on time or that someone is a Mussolini-sympathizer for making the trains run on time.

Such thinking would be an example of the genetic fallacy. However, just because Mussolini made the trains run on time, that does not mean it is fine to sympathize with him, look up to him in general as a counselor, or follow in his path. It is a good thing that Mussolini made the trains run on time, but the monumental evil things he did vastly outweigh the miniscule good that he did.

Answering the question, "What would be your response to those who say that Hitler did some good things?" Pastor Doug Wilson of Christ Church in Moscow, Idaho, responded, "I would say that people who talk that way have completely lost their sense of proportion. They are like those who would say, 'Other than *that*, how was the play, Mrs. Lincoln?'"[70] The level of evil committed by the Nazis is so dark and so extreme that it overshadows any minor, comparatively trivial good that they did.

It makes complete sense that Satan, who masquerades as an angel of light, allowed the Nazis to do a few good things. As with all of Satan's false religions, he mixes in some truth and some goodness with his lies and

---

[70] Wilson, D. (2024, November 25). A Wide-Ranging and Long-Awaited Interview. Blog & Mablog. https://dougwils.com/books-and-culture/s7-engaging-the-culture/inerrant-curiosities.html

wickedness. Satan has nothing good or beautiful to offer anyone. His deceptions would be very unattractive if he did not mix in some of God's truths and goodness. Satan is pleased to create a false religion which promotes the virtue of patriotism, encourages physical health, and makes its people temporarily happier and more materially prosperous, but which is also murderous and sexually perverted.

Without a doubt, it is morally abominable for someone to be a Neo-Nazi or Nazi-Sympathizer since this involves walking in the steps of the wicked, keeping company with them, sympathizing with them, and taking counsel from them. Wolves who advocate this position should not be allowed anywhere near the church. Those who do not repent of their lifestyle of gross sin marked by sympathizing with, following, partnering with, and taking counsel from satanically-inspired perverts, kidnappers, and murderers must be excommunicated from the church, since Christians are not permitted to associate with anyone who lives in gross, unrepentant sin and claims to be a brother (1 Corinthians 5:11).

An Ally to Nazis

So far, the Nazis, Neo-Nazis, and Nazi-sympathizers who agree with much or all of the false doctrines of Nazism could be described as "Side A" Nazis. A "Side B" Nazi, on the other hand, would be someone who personally disagrees with Nazism, but who defends Neo-Nazis and Nazi-sympathizers. A Side B Nazi will say, "Although I personally am not a Nazi and disagree with Nazism, I don't think we should kick Nazis out of our church or go too hard on them. They hold some views which Leftists find offensive, but we shouldn't be opposed to them just because they offend people. A lot of these Nazi guys say that 'Christ is King' and I believe them. And sure, maybe some of them aren't Christians, but our church is for unsaved people too. Can't I love my unsaved children? So it's fine for these guys to belong to our church before they believe."

The problem with a statement like this is that it can also be used to defend almost any other egregious sin. For instance, a Side B pedophile might say of Side A pedophiles: "Although I personally am not a pedophile and I find the idea of pedophilia to be gross, I don't think we should judge people based on their sexual preferences. Lots of people, especially on the Right, are greatly offended by pedophilia, but we shouldn't be opposed to them just because they offend people. The pedophiles I know love kids and love Jesus so much. Maybe some of them aren't Christians yet, but they are welcome at our church. They can have a home here and we won't judge them."

Even though Side B Nazis are not Nazis themselves, they will defend Side A Nazis for one primary reason: they consider Side A Nazis to be on their "team," politically, by virtue of the fact that they have the same enemy, the Left. The Leftists are viewed as such an existential threat to their way of life that they are willing to defend or refuse to criticize anyone who is willing to fight the Leftists alongside them.

In so doing, they (with or without knowing it) practice the political philosophy developed by the Nazi philosopher and jurist, Carl Schmitt, known as the "friend-enemy distinction," proposed in his 1932 book *The Concept of the Political.* This concept teaches that, politically, someone is either your friend or your enemy. Your friends want to preserve your way of life; your enemies want to destroy it. The purpose of politics is to use the power of the state to protect your friends and destroy your enemies. Those who refuse to recognize this principle will be destroyed by their enemies who do understand it, which is why Schmitt was very critical of democratic governments (which allow your enemies to participate in your government) but very supportive of totalitarian governments (which allow for your friends to completely purge your enemies from society).

This Nazi political theory has been pushed recently by none other than Pastor Joel Webbon. After Webbon was exposed for fornicating with a member of his Vineyard church in San Diego in 2012,[71] where Webbon was "one of the youngest ordained Vineyard pastors" and led a congregation of "sixty to seventy people in regular attendance" in "September 2012,"[72] Webbon admitted that the charge of fornication was true.[73] However, Webbon

---

[71] McGowan, E. (2025, March 21). *Fornication, Lies, and Reproach: The Pastoral Ministry of Joel Webbon.* [Article]. X. https://x.com/elimcgowan/status/1903177210988777872

[72] Vineyard Blue Church. (2013, October 14). Our Story. *Internet Archive,* https://web.archive.org/web/20131028163729/http://vineyardblue.org/our-story/

[73] Webbon, J. (2025, March 21). *I wanted to wait to share my response for one simple reason: Because when accusers of the brethren say "jump,"...* [Post]. X. https://x.com/rightresponsem/status/1903222569437892806

attributed the release of this information to revenge for his decision "to publicly address what [he] consider[s] to be a deadly idolatry of Israel and Zionism." Moreover, Webbon observed that the "Friend Enemy Distinction is incredibly real."[74]

This was not the first time Webbon pushed the friend-enemy distinction. In 2024, Webbon stated, "Friend/Enemy - This is a major factor in how I determine alliances."[75] In January 2025, Webbon did a podcast entitled, "Christians Must Crush Their Enemies," where the friend-enemy distinction was promoted. Webbon stated that he was aware that the concept originated with Nazi Carl Schmitt and stated that the friend-enemy distinction is "a good idea. I think it's the way that people behave. Even at minimum, it's a good observation. At maximum, it's a good strategy." Webbon acknowledged that many Christians are uncomfortable with this theory and struggle with it, in

---

[74] McGowan, E. (2025, March 23). *NEW: Webbon says in new Tweet that when he "decided to publicly address what [he] consider[s] to be a deadly...* [Post]. X. https://x.com/elimcgowan/status/1903861710253154318

[75] Webbon, J. (2024, October 22). *The internet is a big place. Unfortunately, I can't keep up with everything. I know nothing about this situation. All...* [Post]. X. https://x.com/rightresponsem/status/1848727695804268684

particular Christian women, with whom Webbon advised his audience to avoid talking about this concept altogether. Webbon encouraged his audience to say, "'I love you sister, could I speak with your husband?' That's what I'd do. Because women aren't fighters and they're not supposed to be. My wife is not a fighter, praise God!"[76]

The friend-enemy distinction completely fails on Biblical grounds, primarily because of Romans 13, which states that the purpose of government is to commend what is good and punish what is evil (Romans 13:3-4). There is no Biblical mandate for governments to dictate and preserve any specific way of life, as Carl Schmitt argued. Instead, governments must protect those who do good and punish those who do evil, regardless of how this affects culture or political alliances. Governments do not get a free pass to shirk punishing evil because the evil is being committed by those who are "friendly" to those in power. Romans 13 does not instruct governments to "bring punishment on the evildoers, unless they are your friends." Similarly, it does not say, "bring punishment on the evildoers, unless this would

---

[76] Webbon, J. (2025, January 7). *The friend-enemy distinction sees politics as defining who preserves or threatens your way of life. Some Christians worry this…* [Video]. X. https://x.com/rightresponsem/status/1876737464171209083

jeopardize the preservation of your way of life or culture." Biblically, the government must punish all evildoers without partiality, because partiality in judgment is abominable to God (James 2:9 and Deuteronomy 1:17).

Throughout history, men have excused their wicked alliances and the sinful things they do by citing past evils that have been done to them, or because of their anxieties about the future. In 1930's Germany, one might have said, "We've got to eradicate the Jewish Communist threat before they eradicate our German way of life!" In South Africa in the 2020's, another might say, "We've got to kill the rich White Boer farmers because of all the evil they have done to our people and because they continue to destroy our African way of life!" A Leftist in the United States might say, "I don't care whether or not my political allies are pedophiles; if the Right gets power, they will destroy our liberal democracy and way of life!"

It doesn't matter whether someone is on the same political side or whether you personally aren't bothered by their sin. The Word of God is clear that you must not associate with those who claim to be Christians but who live lives of gross sin (1 Corinthians 5:11), which certainly describes Side A Nazis and Side A pedophiles. Their political affiliation does not matter when it comes to obeying God.

If you are a Side B Nazi because you are secretly attracted to Nazism, this is equally as dangerous as if you were attracted to pedophilia. Nazism is a murderous, idolatrous ideology and, as we have seen, "Hitler lovers" are not afraid to advocate for abolishing the age of consent and marrying children who have just become fertile. So, this is a temptation that you must refuse, for the sake of your soul. The first step in defeating this temptation is to stop defending Nazis and instead publicly call out the sin of these perverts and distance yourself from all those who practice it.

Seeker-Sensitive Churches

It is also vital for Christian churches to not be "seeker-sensitive." This occurs primarily in politically extreme Left and Right-wing churches which are concerned about creating a church environment that is welcoming to sinners, without calling these sinners to repentance. Sometimes, these churches are fairly open about the fact that they will never preach sermons against or confront individuals about their sins of fornication, perversion, Nazism, or racism. Other times, pastors from these churches claim that they will confront these sins eventually on an individual level, but in the meantime they need to create a welcoming church home for the sinners and bring the sinners to Jesus first. But rarely do they ever get around to seriously confronting these gross sins, let alone excommunicating those who remain unrepentant. Seeker-sensitive teaching is contrary to the Word of God and very dangerous to the church and the soul of the sinner.

If a Nazi or pedophile comes to a church and claims to be a follower of Jesus, he must be rebuked and forbidden from returning until he repents. The church must not associate with such a person (1 Corinthians 5:11). If they welcome him into the fold, there is a very real risk that his sin will spread in the church like cancer.

If a Nazi or pedophile does not claim to be a Christian, the church must still confront him over his sin and preach repentance to him, but an environment which is welcoming of his sin should not be created. In Corinthians 14:24-25, Paul says,

But if all prophesy, and an unbeliever or an ungifted man enters, he is convicted by all, he is called to account by all; the secrets of his heart are disclosed; and so he will fall on his face and worship God, declaring that God is certainly among you.

Although this passage is part of a section that is talking about speaking in tongues and prophecy, it makes clear that it is a good thing for unbelievers to be convicted of their sin by the Word of God which will disclose the secrets of the heart (Hebrews 4:12) as soon as they set foot in the church. If the sinner is truly convicted of his Nazi or pedophilic sin and repents after being confronted by the powerful Word of God, then you know that he has been chosen by God (1 Thessalonians 1:4-5) and can welcome him as a member of the church. If he is offended by the truth about his sin being preached to him and leaves, then he should not be in church convincing himself that he is saved when he is not.

As a pastor, if you allow an unbeliever to attend your church without ever seriously preaching the truth to him about his sin, his soul will be in a much more dangerous position than if he never went to church in the first place. He will begin to believe that he is a Christian and that he is saved when, in fact, he is not. His belief that he is saved will make it much harder for him to ever repent of his sin and truly accept salvation.

Pastors are responsible to God for watching over the souls of those who are in their church or who are influenced by their ministry (Hebrews 13:17). If a pastor refuses to preach the truth to the souls of hellbound sinners who God has placed in his care, this is a dereliction of duty and he will answer to God for what he has done. Such a pastor, like a wolf, does not care about the sheep, but only cares about being respected and making money from his followers.

Pastors who tolerate Nazi false doctrines in their church (or worse yet, promote this heresy) because all the young Right-wing men are becoming Nazi-sympathizers are no different than King Rehoboam, who rejected the wise advice of the elders and opted for the rash and foolish advice of the young men (1 Kings 12 and 2 Chronicles 10). Pastors who reject the wisdom of our staunchly anti-Nazi elders and fathers and side with increasingly Nazi-sympathizing young men will bring as much division and ruin to the church as King Rehoboam brought to Israel.

Side B Nazis often believe there is nothing wrong with them defending Nazis or treating Nazism as something that is not a big deal. After all, they aren't Nazis themselves. However, one of the biggest problems with being a Side B Nazi is the danger which you pose to your children and grandchildren. For the pastor or spiritual father, this danger will be to your spiritual children.

It is common for parents who defend Nazism to cause their children to become Nazis. The children see their parents constantly defending Nazis and racists and, in so doing, bestowing honor on Nazis and racists. Because of this, they conclude that their parents will defend them and honor them if they become a Nazi or a racist. In fact, they will see this as the quickest and easiest way of getting respect and affirmation, which they so desperately crave, from their parents.

Likewise, if they see their parents apathetically treating Nazism and racism as something unimportant, they will conclude that there is nothing wrong with becoming Nazi or racist themselves. Their parents won't care, since they clearly don't care when anyone else does it. You may not think you are hurting anyone (especially because you are not a Nazi yourself), but by defending Nazis or being apathetic towards their sin, you are significantly increasing the risk that your children, who are closely watching your words and actions, will become full-blown Neo-Nazis, Nazi-sympathizers, or racists.

Common Objections

There are two common objections to what I have discussed here that need to be quickly addressed before moving on. First, some conservatives say that the only people who call out Nazism today are Leftists. This is an excellent example of an ad hominem logic fallacy and could be dismissed for that reason alone. However, it is also not true. There are many Christians who are generally conservative, but deeply opposed to Nazism *because it is evil.* This is the same reason why someone should be opposed to Communism and pedophilia; not because Communists and pedophiles are our political enemies, but because these things are evil.

If someone uses the label "Leftist" as an insult against those who oppose Nazism, it is probably because he understands that Leftism has many moral failings. However, the same Bible which condemns many tenets of Leftism condemns even more tenets of Nazism. So, if someone justifies or defends Nazism or Nazis, he has no grounds to be morally opposed to Leftism or Leftists or to insult others by suggesting that they must be Leftists if they are opposed to Nazism.

Additionally, saying that Nazism should not be opposed because the majority of people who do oppose it are Leftists indicates that the person making this statement is a Side B Nazi. This person shields Nazis from criticism, since he and the Nazis are on the same political team and share a common political enemy. As a hyper-partisan Right-wing loyalist, he believes the Leftists to be his only true enemies and, by extension, the only true enemies of anyone who falls on the right. He actually thinks he can defeat those who have arguments against the Nazis by simply implying that they are Leftists, a label he would be appalled to receive himself. But to those who oppose evil wherever it is found on the political spectrum, such an objection means little.

Lastly, other conservatives complain that they are "sick and tired" of a "ten year period of human history" (World War II) and the "game between Nazis and Jews" being constantly "relitigated." This is an extremely concerning take. First, it is not primarily the Left who are "relitigating" the "ten years" of "Nazis vs. Jews." There are numerous self-labeled Nazis and Nazi-sympathizers on the Right who are trying to relitigate the drama that played out in World War II (for example, by doing very long podcasts about how America was on the wrong side of the conflict; how Churchill was the greatest villain of the War; or how the "post-war-consensus" has destroyed the West) and who are pushing Nazi propaganda about race and the Jews. They are the ones who are literally "relitigating" this issue. For about seventy-five years, almost everyone was fine with the outcome of World War II. Now, these Woke Right influencers have decided to challenge it. If they did not bring these topics up and push these Nazi false doctrines, there would be no need for us to defend against them.

Additionally, the events that happened in Nazi Germany before and during World War II are not an isolated occurrence of history. They are part of two different patterns which have played out over and over again for thousands of years. First, Nazi Germany is an excellent example of the innumerable nations throughout history which fell into moral decline and degeneracy and then, instead of repenting of their sins, sought salvation in totalitarianism and monarchy. If this pattern is being observed in Western nations today, it is reasonable for students of history to highlight similarities and make comparisons between Western nations and other nations to which this has happened (e.g., Nazi Germany). God gave us records of history in part so that we could learn from the mistakes of those who came before us.

Second, Nazi Germany is one of many nations which Satan has used throughout history in his attempt to exterminate the Jews. The lies told about the Jews in Nazi Germany were many of the same lies that former Satanic empires used to justify persecuting the Jews (e.g., the Egyptians, Persians, Seleucids, Romans, Spanish, Soviets, various medieval nations, etc.) and are some of the same lies which are being told in Western nations today. There is nothing wrong with learning from Satan's schemes and lies of the past so that you can more effectively fight them in the present, especially since he tends to use the same lies, or variations of the same lies, over and over again. It is completely fine for someone who is familiar with history to draw parallels and say, "these are the same lies that were told in Nazi Germany" or "this is a tired lie that was used in the Soviet Union" and then show how the Nazis and the Soviets got it wrong and what lessons we can learn from them.

To conclude this chapter, I have one very important final note. If you are the godly Christian wife of a husband who is becoming radicalized by Nazi ideology, then I would encourage you to read the story of Abigail, Nabal, and David, which can be found in 1 Samuel 25. Abigail was an intelligent, godly woman who had a husband who was a reckless fool. Nabal rashly and unnecessarily offended David, who then planned to kill Nabal. Abigail, however, wisely went behind her husband's back by going to David and interceding for mercy on behalf of her foolish husband.

If your husband is becoming a Nazi, it is incredibly foolish, reckless, and evil, and will bring danger to your husband and your family's souls. If it is safe for you to confront him, you should tell him, "No, I am not going there with you." If he doesn't listen to you, or if it is not safe to confront him, then you need to go behind his back and against his wishes, if necessary, to get help. You need to discreetly send up a signal flare so that other competent saints know that your family is in trouble and can come to your—and, ultimately, his—aid. Find a competent, trustworthy pastor or wise person in your congregation who will be able to help you in rescuing your foolish husband from the cliff that he is about to step off.

The Swastika in the Sanctuary

Chapter III: Woke Right Ideology

Since the race riots of 2020, many Christians have become acutely aware of the threat to the church posed by Woke Left ideology. However, ever since the October 7, 2023, terror massacre of Israeli Jews, antisemitism, racism, and critical theories on the *Right* have exploded in popularity, causing many Christians to realize that a Woke *Right* also exists and threatens the church.

So what exactly is Woke ideology? Ultimately, it is nothing more than repackaged tenets of National *Socialist* (Nazi) doctrine. Those who subscribe to socialistic worldviews (whether they are Nazis or Communists) hold to a "critical theory" which means that they see the world through the lens of a power struggle between a dominant class and an oppressed class. This sociological theory originated in the 1920's at the Frankfurt School of Philosophy in Germany and was greatly influenced by the writings of Karl Marx.

Unsurprisingly, critical theory has been used throughout the last hundred years chiefly as a tool for tyrants to manipulate their populations into starting revolutions which result in totalitarianism. Although critical theories have *primarily* been used by Communists, they are not inherently Communist and can be used to instigate societal conflict for the purpose of establishing any kind of totalitarian regime, which is exactly how Hitler came into power. Critical theories are also not intrinsically racist, although they tend to be very racist today. Originally, most critical theories focused on the struggle for power between wealthy capitalists (the dominant class) and the common worker (the oppressed class). However, when critical theories are adopted in nations which have tumultuous race relations, race will inevitably become incorporated into the theory.

Defining Right and Left

Before we can look at the differences and similarities between the Woke Left and the Woke Right, it is important to clarify what the definitions of "Right" and "Left" are, since this is a frequent point of contention among hyper-partisans who are uncomfortable with the idea that bad people exist on on their side of the political aisle. Commonly,

Right and Left are viewed by people in terms of stances on issues (e.g., the Right opposes immigration and the Left supports it). This definition is acceptable for day-to-day conversation and surface-level discussions, but it does not sufficiently convey the full meaning of these terms, which is necessary for any kind of sophisticated study.

The issues that Right and Left support frequently change and reverse. For instance, in the early 2000s, the Right in America was pro-war, while the Left was anti-war; less than twenty years later during the Biden Administration, the Left became pro-war while the Right became anti-war. Today, under the Trump administration, it is quite possible that the two sides could flip again soon on this issue. So, Right and Left cannot be determined purely based on political stances or issues. Furthermore, it is common for Right and Left to agree on some issues (for example, the most extreme sides of the Right and Left both hate Israel and the Jews), meaning that the definition of Right and Left also can't be explained in terms of them taking opposite positions.

The definition of Right and Left which has the most explanatory power sociologically is the following: the Right prefers to conserve or reinstitute the old ways, while the Left prefers to usher in new ways. The national socialist seeks to institute totalitarianism and commit genocide to make Germany great and strong *again*, while the international socialist seeks to institute totalitarianism and commit genocide to usher in a *new* Communist utopia.

On the issue of war, the Right supported war two decades ago because it was seen as a way of conserving America's pride and dominance over the world. As of the writing of this book, the Right now opposes war because of their desire to conserve the American way of life, which will inevitably be jeopardized if a world war breaks out at this time. The Left opposed war twenty years ago because they wanted America to stop being the "world's policeman," a new idea which they believed would liberate the world from American interference. Recently, the Left began to support war as a means of freeing the world from Russian oppression with the ultimate hope of ushering in a new democracy in Russia.

This definition also explains why the Right trails the Left on many issues. The Left creates apparent new realities that a nation and the world begin to internalize (legalized abortion or gay marriage for instance). After these realities have been established for a long period of time, however, the Right comes to support these positions, since they are old. For example, in the United States, the Right is currently in the process of pivoting to become pro-abortion and pro-homosexuality, especially after the 2024 election when Donald Trump promoted abortion and gay marriage with the continued support and approval of the Right; this is happening because abortion and homosexuality have been legally practiced in America for a long time now. Eventually, the Left will then come to oppose the "old" positions protected by the Right and create "new" realities, and the cycle of human history repeats.

Based on this discussion, it should be obvious that being politically Right or Left is not fundamentally morally preferable. Sometimes the Right is correct on an issue and sometimes the Left is. Then, in five, twenty, or a hundred years the two sides will flip on the position and so will the side which is morally correct on that issue. Each issue advocated for by the Right and Left must be evaluated to see whether it aligns with the Word of God. If the Right is currently on the correct side of the abortion issue,

Biblically-speaking, you should align with the Right on that issue. If the Right is currently on the wrong side of the immigration issue, Biblically-speaking, you should not align with the Right on that issue. Your political affiliation does not give you an excuse to violate the Word of God. If you place your political affiliation above God's word, it has become a true idol.

Right and Left Both Gone Woke

With this nuance explained, the similarities and differences between the Woke Right and Woke Left can now be examined. The Woke Left has awakened to a critical theory which sees the world in terms of a power struggle between a dominant class (Whites, men, Christians, Jews, traditional families, fascists, racists, Zionists, capitalists, and the political establishment) and an oppressed class (Blacks, other racial and ethnic minorities, Muslims, LGBTQ individuals, and practitioners of American, African, and Asian pagan religions).

The Woke Right has also awakened to a critical theory which sees the world in terms of a power struggle between a dominant class (Racial and ethnic minorities, women, Jews, Communists, Zionists, globalists, and the political establishment) and an oppressed class (Whites, men, cultural Christians, "heritage Americans," traditional families, Nazi sympathizers, Holocaust deniers, anti-Semites, racists, anti-feminists, and those who practice European pagan religions). The Woke Right does not like for the terms "dominant class," "oppressed class," or "critical theory" to be applied to their beliefs. But this is an accurate representation of what they believe.

As you can see, Woke Right and Woke Left have some perceived enemies in common (e.g., Jews and Zionists). But, when it comes to their belief on who the members of the oppressed class are, they currently have almost exactly inverted beliefs. Another important thing to note is that not everyone who is Woke Left is transgender or an African pagan and not everyone who is Woke Right is a Nazi-sympathizer or racist. However, everyone who is Woke Left will defend (or, at a minimum, refuse to criticize) transgender individuals or African pagans; in the same way, everyone who is Woke Right will defend (or, at a minimum, refuse to criticize) Nazi-sympathizers and racists. This is because of the belief that victims should not oppress other victims and should be united in their fight against the oppressive class.

Interestingly, both the Woke Right and the Woke Left have a semi-established priority structure for determining who is the most oppressed—and whoever is the most oppressed gets the loudest voice and is exempt from criticism. With the Woke Left, a Black woman is more oppressed than a White man and gets more of a say. However, a White trans man is more oppressed than a straight Black woman and can't be criticized by the Black woman. Currently, the most oppressed category of individuals are Black trans women who are practitioners of African pagan religions.

With the Woke Right, a White man is more oppressed than a Black woman and is entitled to more of a say because of this. But, a Black woman who is a Nazi-sympathizer and anti-Semite is more oppressed and gets more of a voice than a White man who is not a Nazi-sympathizer or anti-Semite. Currently, the most oppressed category of individuals within the Woke Right are White straight men with large traditional families who are Nazi-sympathizers, racists, anti-feminists, and anti-Semites who practice cultural Christianity or European paganism.

To illustrate how this phenomenon plays out, it is common for those on the Woke Right to criticize White, conservative women podcasters or influencers and tell them that they need to go home and speak truth only to their children. However, they will publicly praise and seek an appearance on the show of a Black woman podcaster who is a notorious anti-Semite and Nazi-sympathizer. Even though she is a Black woman and women are supposed to stay home, the fact that she is an anti-Semite and Nazi-sympathizer makes her very "cool" and entitles her to having a voice and a platform.

Those who hold to Woke critical theories cannot acknowledge that their theories fail to account for more oppressor and oppressed classes than their theories allow. For instance, members of the Woke Left fiercely oppose the phrase "all lives matter" when it is in contrast with "Black lives matter." Although "all lives matter" should be an uncontroversial statement, it triggers the Woke Left because it implies that people other than Blacks have been oppressed. To the Woke Left, the oppression of Blacks cannot be compared to any other group. The Woke Left also cannot tolerate the idea that Blacks could oppress others.

This same principle plays out on the Woke Right as well. In response to a video of a South African political leader allegedly shouting "Kill the Boer," Pastor Joel Webbon posted the following prayer on X:

> Dear God, In your mercy, grant these people, made in your image, true repentance. If not, then in your justice, destroy all those who perpetuate the only genuine form of widespread racism in the world today - envious, unjustifiable hatred toward white people. Amen.[77]

Such a statement is obviously absurd considering how much widespread, murderous racial and ethnic partiality exists in the world today, especially against the Jews, Kurds, Armenians, Yazidis, Uyghurs, Pygmies, Rohingya, and Tigrayans. For some of these racial and ethnic groups, violent genocides are being carried out against nearly every member of the group, which cannot be said about the overwhelming majority of White people in the world. But

---

[77] Webbon, J. (2025, February 9). *Dear God, In your mercy, grant these people, made in your image, true repentance. If not, then in your justice...* [Post]. X.
https://x.com/rightresponsem/status/1888679996589486456

those who hold critical theories on the Woke Right and the Woke Left do not care about the truth; the only thing they care about is their status as absolute victims and their desire to take power from their perceived oppressors and execute vengeance on them.

In 2017, conservative political influencer Matt Walsh wrote about the similarities between far-left and far-right extremists which he observed following the protests and clashes in Charlottesville. I am not sure whether or not Walsh would still agree with these words that he wrote almost a decade ago, but they are very insightful:

[…] You will notice one thing as our death spirals get faster and faster: the terrorists on both sides will become ever more indistinguishable. As they clash with one another in the streets, it will be hard to tell one from the other. The only thing that will mark them as distinct is the flag they carry. But apart from that swastika or that hammer and sickle, they will be -- and currently are -- virtually identical.

Indeed, the similarities between the alt-right white supremacist and the leftist Antifa thug are impossible to miss:

-They are both obsessed with identity politics.

-They are both racist.

-They are both fascist authoritarians who care more about dominating the opposition than protecting the freedoms of all Americans.

-They are both lonely and desperate for attention.

-They are both nihilists.

-They both lack purpose or direction in their lives.

-They are both morally defective.

-They both could have used stronger male role models growing up.

-They both are driven by equal parts hatred and boredom.

And so on.[78]

---

[78] Walsh, M. (2017, August 14). Matt Walsh: Dear alt-right white supremacists and leftist Antifa thugs, you deserve each other. Blaze Media.
https://www.theblaze.com/contributions/matt-walsh-dear-alt-right-white-supremacists-and-leftist-antifa-thugs-you-deserve-each-other

Selected Quotes

If you are not witnessing the change actively occurring in Christian, Right-wing social media and teaching, you may desire additional proof that the Woke Right to which I have been referring exists. Although there is an incomprehensible amount of evidence for their existence on X alone which anyone can easily find, I have provided some quotes below from major influencers which you can judge for yourself and determine if they are the same things that I have been talking about here.

Nick Fuentes had this to say: "I feel like the last person alive who is still J-Woke, pro-White, traditional Christian, and anti-feminist—in a word: REDPILLED"[79] (where "J-Woke" appears to be a reference to "woke about the Jews").

Stephen Wolfe, author of *The Case for Christian Nationalism*, wrote the following in his book:

Every step of progress is overcoming you. Ask yourself, "What sort of villain does each event of

---

[79] Fuentes, N. (2024, December 17). *I feel like the last person alive who is still J-Woke, pro-White, traditional Christian, and anti-feminist— in a word: REDPILLED.* [Post]. X. https://x.com/NickJFuentes/status/1869121804150911216

progress have in common?" The straight white male. That is the chief out-group of New America, the embodiment of regression and oppression.[80]

In the same book, Wolfe also stated:

We live under a gynocracy—a rule by women. This may not be apparent on the surface, since men still run many things. But the governing virtues of America are feminine vices, associated with certain feminine virtues, such as empathy, fairness, and equality.[81]

Later, Wolfe further stated,

If you are a white, heterosexual, cis-gendered male, then the world will not offer you any favors. Indeed, your career advancement depends on sacrificing your self-respect by praising and pandering to your inferiors who rule over you.[82]

Wolfe even admitted on X that he holds to a critical theory:

Anti-woke Christians, in their rejection of "power hierarchies" and "privilege," have rendered

---

[80] Wolfe, S. (2022). *The Case for Christian Nationalism.* Pg. 436. Canon Press.
[81] Ibid, pg. 448.
[82] Ibid, pg. 464.

themselves incapable of seeing the absurd but real privileges and power hierarchy at work in our world[…] This is why I will not reject a "critical" approach to social phenomena. There are subtle hierarchies of power, some natural and proper, and others artificial and absurd.[83,84]

Additionally, Wolfe stated, "I fully admit that if being a 'conservative' requires one to reject a 'critical' approach to social phenomena, then I'm not a conservative."[85] This statement made by Wolfe was in response to someone who quoted Wolfe as previously saying, "I am not conservative because I agree in part with the 'critical' methodology of the left, but come to different conclusions and valuations."[86]

---

[83] Wolfe, S. (2023, March 31). *Anti-woke Christians, in their rejection of "power hierarchies" and "privilege," have rendered themselves incapable of seeing the absurd but real*... [Post]. X. https://x.com/PerfInjust/status/1641824897721614338

[84] Wolfe, S. (2023, March 31). *This is why I will not reject a "critical" approach to social phenomena. There are subtle hierarchies of power, some*... [Post]. X. https://x.com/PerfInjust/status/1641825496802512898

[85] Wolfe, S. (2023, July 7). *I fully admit that if being a "conservative" requires one to reject a "critical" approach to social phenomena, then I'm not*... [Post]. X. https://x.com/PerfInjust/status/1677465088276439041

[86] Wokal Distance. (2023, July 7). *I am not conservative because I agree in part with the "critical" methodology of the left, but come to different*... [Image showing a post made by Stephen Wolfe, containing the previous quote]. X. https://x.com/wokal_distance/status/1677457029722705920

As another example, Pastor Joel Webbon shared a video showing clips of Blacks, Jews, and other non-Whites behaving badly followed by a cringe hype montage glorifying members of the White race, including footage of German soldiers, Patriot Front members, American Nazi Party founder George Lincoln Rockwell, Corey Mahler, and Webbon himself. Webbon included the following message with this video:

> Communists, Immigrants, Muslims, Jews, and Transgenders have all declared war on our country. And the Kosher Right continues to shoot anyone who says something about it in the back. Enough is enough.[87]

This is not the first concerning statement made by Webbon. Another quote from Webbon which appears to display this type of identity politics is the following:

> Like, I walk around my neighborhood, and it's not that there are different shades of, you know, white and brown... Who cares? No, it's, I mean, full, straight-up Hindu garb at our neighborhood

[87] Webbon, J. (2025, September 11). *Communists, Immigrants, Muslims, Jews, and Transgenders have all declared war on our country. And the Kosher Right continues to shoot...* [Post]. X.
https://x.com/rightresponsem/status/1966298785212149843

swimming pool that my daughter is asking and I'm trying to explain… And I don't even know what country I'm in, in my own neighborhood. I just, I don't know where I am… When we go on a family walk, the number of Pakistani, Hindu, all these different, not just ethnicities, but religions with visible religious outfits on. And, you know the same thing when we go to Costco, I'm like where, where am I?... It's rare, like we'll go on a family walk and every now and then we'll pass by a White family that's a man and a woman and has more than one kid. And every time I see it, I'm like, I don't want to be this way, but I feel like this, like, small sense of relief, like "I see you. I'm glad you're one of my neighbors." Because at the end of the day, again, it's not about Whiteness; but at the end of the day, if things get rough, I don't know if my Hindu neighbor is going to fight to save the lives of my children.[88]

Although Webbon gave the impression that his observations are based on religion (by referencing Hindus),

---

[88] Spare No Arrows. (2025, January 2). *Joel Webbon | Wolf or The Best Evangelicalism Has To Offer?* [Video]. YouTube. https://www.youtube.com/watch?v=Omj_21qxHkM&t=227s

this appeared to be false to some who paid attention to what he said. First, Webbon slipped up and included "Pakistani" individuals in his list of outsiders who he didn't trust and was then forced to clarify that it was "not just [other] ethnicities" that he was worried about.

Second, dressing according to the customs and dress codes of India does not automatically make you Hindu. Despite Webbon's apparent belief that he can do this, you cannot look at someone wearing clothing that is typically worn in day-to-day life in India (including by Christians in India) and assume that a person is Hindu. More than likely, if Webbon met a Christian from India who was dressed like an Indian, Webbon would assume that she was a Hindu, based upon what he said here; unless, of course, he does not actually care about religion as much as he does about race and ethnicity.

Third, Joel did not make any mention about the religion of the White family who he believed, just by looking at them, would fight to save his kids. Joel claimed that it was not about "Whiteness," but provided no other description other than saying that the family consists of a man and woman and more than one kid. It is entirely possible that a

White family like this could be heathen Communists who hate conservatives like Joel and his kids; on the other hand, a Pakistani family who dresses according to their native culture could be Christian, conservative, and willing to fight to save America if we were invaded. Despite the attempts that were made to avoid this claim, it appears that racial and ethnic identity politics (where certain races or ethnicities are presumed to be on your side, while others are presumed to be against your side, simply because of their race or ethnicity) is suffused in Webbon's statement here.

In 2025, Webbon preached the following from the pulpit of his church:

> It is actually a benefit when there is an aristocracy, whether formally or informally, meaning when there is a class of citizens that is a subset of the population as a whole that have been groomed and trained rigorously in virtue, in intellect, in philosophy, and most importantly the Scriptures and that they would be appointed to lead, and the peanut gallery wouldn't. "But our sacred democracy!" You know why Democrats love democracy so much? Because only when you have universal suffrage do you get a

Democrat elected. It is only when you get the lowest IQ population, the poorest population, the highest statistically-criminalized population, and give them an equal vote with Heritage Americans who have been here for four-hundred years, who work hard, who pay the bulk of the taxes, and who are outstanding citizens who have not broken the law—it is only when you make everyone else an equal voter to them that you get someone like Ilhan Omar in a political office.[89]

Which demographic of the population is it that certain evil men constantly point out is the lowest IQ, poorest, and highest statistically-criminalized? Let the reader analyze Webbon's statement here and form his own conclusions about which demographic of the population he is advocating to deny equal voting rights to.

Webbon's comments here are almost laughably absurd. The Democrats were elected to public office for nearly a hundred years by men before women were given the right to vote with universal suffrage. Also, the vast majority

---

[89] Right Response Ministries. (2025, March 11). *"Inferiors & Superiors"* [Video]. YouTube. https://www.youtube.com/watch?v=4Tn2aRfRPWk&t=599s

of voters in Vermont would likely meet whatever Webbon's definition of a "Heritage American" is. It is one of the Whitest states in the country, likely with far more residents who can trace their ancestry back to colonial America than residents of other states, and presumably it has a very small amount of whatever demographic is "the lowest IQ, poorest, and highest statistically-criminalized." Yet, Vermont is also one of the most Democrat states in the nation.

Webbon demonstrated more of the identity politics described in this chapter in a podcast he did in August 2025, where he described the four pillars necessary "to save America": "Christianity, Patriarchy, Anti-Zionist, Race-Realist."[90] Race-realism is the belief that certain races are not only genetically superior or inferior to other races, but morally superior or inferior as well. This will be discussed more later in this chapter, but the belief that race realism, along with patriarchy and anti-Zionism, is necessary to save America, is a perfect example of critical theory and identity politics.

Webbon demonstrated more of his anti-woman identity politics when he stated,

---

[90] Right Response Ministries. (2025, August 8). *Four Pillars to Save America*. [Video]. YouTube. https://www.youtube.com/live/pz8INi4N0lg

In a nutshell, in general, I don't want to see women in the public sphere. You mean, they shouldn't hold political office? Correct. You mean, you don't want to see them podcasting? Correct. But, what about in the marketplace, you know, with nine-to-five careers? No, not that either. I don't want to see women holding positions in the public square... I don't.[91]

In another display of these anti-female identity politics, Webbon indicated that the primary reason he does not like Attorney General Pam Bondi is not because of her policies, but because of her gender, during a message that he preached from his pulpit:

When you say, "Well, I don't think that um... Well I disagree with uh... Pam Bondi, because I think she's hiding the Epstein files." And, I'd be like, yeah, but also I don't like Pam Bondi because she's a woman... and she shouldn't be in public. Not in politics. You know, like the meme that's like, "You and I are not the same. You don't like her for this reason. I don't like..." It's like, "Oh I don't like Pam Bondi because

[91] Mantyla, K. (2025, March 5). Joel Webbon Does Not Want To See Women In The Public Sphere. People for the American Way. [Video]. https://www.peoplefor.org/rightwingwatch/joel-webbon-does-not-want-se e-women-public-sphere

of her positions." And I'm like, "I don't like Pam Bondi because she needs to be at home."[92]

In July 2025, Webbon shared a picture of a page of a book that made the claim that a 1921 Maine Supreme Court ruling, *State vs. Mockus*, made it illegal to spread Jewish or Talmudic propaganda.[93] The title of the book, which Webbon did not advertise in his post, but was easily discovered, is *America: Free, White, & Christian* by Charles Weisman, a heretical "Christian Identity" movement author.[94] In his books *The Origin of Race and Civilization* and *Who is Esau-Edom?* this same author argues that White Europeans are the true Israel; that Jesus did not come to save races other than White Europeans;[95] that the Jews are predetermined by

---

[92] Right Wing Watch. (2025, July 15). *Misogynistic Christian nationalist pastor Joel Webbon explains that he doesn't oppose Attorney General Pam Bondi because she's hiding the Epstein...* [Post with video from a sermon Joel Webbon preached]. X. https://x.com/RightWingWatch/status/1945147400923886002

[93] Hitler Hated Christ. (2025, July 1). *1) The state of Maine, as recently as 1921, determined that America was a "Christian land." 2) They also determined it...* [Image showing a post made by Joel Webbon, containing the previous quote]. X. https://x.com/not_our_guy/status/1940150249621684495

[94] Hitler Hated Christ. (2025, July 1). *So apparently Webbon is citing "christian identity" authors now.* [Post and images of the book Joel Webbon posted a picture from]. X. https://x.com/not_our_guy/status/1940181000174346511

[95] Hitler Hated Christ. (2025, July 1). *More from the "christian identity" author referenced by Joel Webbon in his advocating for blasphemy laws*

their genetics to kill all White people and that it is impossible for them to not be evil;[96] and that, "The Negro, Oriental and Tasmanian were not made in the image of God, were not written in the Book of Life, and will never be resurrected."[97]

Even Christian musician Brian Sauvé has evidently decided to play the identity politics game, as illustrated by the following quote:

> Yes, the Civil Rights Act of 1964 [which ended segregation in the United States] was a mistake. When you see a thug with a rap sheet a mile long slitting a young girl's throat on a subway, you're seeing the ten-thousandth reason why.[98]

If racial segregation was permitted in the United States again, this would not prevent women and children from being at risk of violence in public. White people do evil

---

against "Jewish Propaganda" >White... [Post]. X.
https://x.com/not_our_guy/status/1940220881592271149

[96] Hitler Hated Christ. (2025, July 1). *Same author on how Jews are genetically predetermined to attempt to kill all Whites and that they are incapable of...* [Post]. X.
https://x.com/not_our_guy/status/1940222763282952407

[97] Hitler Hated Christ. (2025, July 1). *Author explaining that Negros are not "adamic" and that Christ didn't come to redeem them. "The Negro, Oriental and Tasmanian...* [Post]. X.
https://x.com/not_our_guy/status/1940223998589378900

[98] Sauvé, B. (2025, September 12). *Yes, the Civil Rights Act of 1964 was a mistake. When you see a thug with a rap sheet...* [Post]. X.
https://x.com/Brian_Sauve/status/1966525411141263468

things too. In 2018, a White man, John Cowell, randomly murdered a Black woman at a train station by stabbing her to death, a crime which he was convicted of.[99] In August 2025, a White man is alleged to have attacked a random woman who he was sitting behind on a Tulsa bus by slitting her throat.[100] Additionally, on September 10, 2025, the same day as the Charlie Kirk assassination (which was also perpetrated by a White man), a White teenage male who was radicalized online and expressed Neo-Nazi views shot two students at a high school in Colorado before turning the gun on himself.[101] There are too many acts of violence like this to list, let alone the many incidents of terrorism where hundreds of women and children were murdered by White men like Dylann Roof, Payton Gendron, and Timothy McVeigh.

---

[99] Convicted Killer John Lee Cowell Sentenced To Life In Fatal BART Station Stabbing Of Nia Wilson. (2020, July 17). CBS San Francisco. https://www.cbsnews.com/sanfrancisco/news/convicted-killer-john-lee-c owell-set-for-sentencing-in-fatal-bart-station-stabbing-of-nia-wilson/

[100] Ledbetter, R. (2025, August 4). Tulsa Police arrest man following random knife attack on city bus: 'It's seemingly random'. News 9. https://www.news9.com/story/689126bf0b51a53dd5ce96a3/tulsa-bus-sta bbing-random-attack-suspect-arrest-robert-rhoades

[101] Evergreen High School Shooter's Online Activity Reveals Fascination with Mass Shootings, White Supremacy (2025, September 12). Anti-Defamation League. https://www.adl.org/resources/article/evergreen-high-school-shooters-onl ine-activity-reveals-fascination-mass-shootings

Some may try to argue that primarily only *Leftist* White men would behave violently. However, not only were several of the individuals that I used as examples here White men on the Right, but even the CATO Institute (which is not a Leftist organization) published a study showing that the Right, including White supremacy groups, have committed a significantly higher number of politically-motivated murders (395) than the Left (65) since 1975 in the United States.[102] Even since 2020, the Right has been responsible for more politically-motivated murders than the Left and all other ideologies combined.[103] Because all races, regardless of what partisan political beliefs they hold to, are deeply sinful and violent, the reinstitution of racial segregation in America would not protect women or children.

Another example of identity politics for the reader to examine is the following statement made by C. Jay Engel, a self-described "Heritage American" and Christian political influencer:

---

[102] Nowrasteh, A. (2025, September 11). Politically Motivated Violence Is Rare in the United States. CATO Institute. https://www.cato.org/blog/politically-motivated-violence-rare-united-states

[103] Ibid.

When I say Heritage American, this is what I mean: those who are ethno-culturally tied to the ethos and spirit of the United States prior to its definitional transformation into a Propositional Nation after World War II. This therefore includes the type of people that came here during the Ellis Island generation, even if that was a significant sociopolitical mistake. We are also the product of our mistakes as a nation. It includes the blacks of the Old South (like Booker T Washington), though it repudiates any instinct that some of them have to leverage their experience for the purposes of political guilt in our time. It also includes integrated Native Americans with the same stipulation. It affirms however the domination and pre-eminence of the European derived peoples, their institutions, and their way of life. Heritage America is centered around the experiences and norms of Anglo-Protestants. It was their customs, their instincts, their priorities, their norms, their struggles, their perspectives, that set the tone and vision of Heritage America. Anything outside of that either assimilated or was killed off. [...]

Heritage America has strong ethnic, correlations—and even types of hierarchies— but it is not racially essentialist in an absolutist way (after all we are not social rationalists). However, I should also note that this does not preclude any ethnic consciousness that might be necessary to confront the ethnic consciousness of the left in their own definition of friends and enemies... Heritage America, of course, is most consistent with anglo Protestantism. But that does not mean that all groups outside of that core are equally dangerous to it. There is a spectrum at play wherein some peoples are less threatening to its ethos than others. There is a high correlation between that spectrum and the broadening circles extending out from Western Europe. Such that peoples like Indians, or South East Asians or Ecuadorians or immigrated Africans are the least capable of fitting in and should be sent home immediately. Whereas groups, like Irish or Italians or Catholics may not fit the original core, but were closer on the spectrum, being Europeans. All politics is contextual and situational.[104]

And how should we remove these people, who are not Heritage Americans, from American society? In a September 2025 X post, Engel stated that he believes violence and breaking the law, including suspending the U.S. Constitution, is needed:

> […] If we want to reverse this stuff, technical mechanisms like deportations and remigration and immigration caps are not what is required. That's misleading.
>
> It would have been true in 2000. But it's 2025. If you want to reverse this stuff, you have to redefine the Postwar Consensus definition on things like unbounded religious liberty, absolutist individual rights, and a universalist version of equal representation. You have to ignore the legal edifice of the postwar federal framework.
>
> These are US citizens in Dearborn. You would have to denaturalize, strip people of their

---

[104] Engel, C. (2024, May 26). *When I say Heritage American, this is what I mean: those who are ethno-culturally tied to the ethos and spirit…* [Post]. X. https://x.com/contramordor/status/1794811572684263627

citizenship, forcibly remove them from their second and third generation homes. It would require violence. You'd have to ignore courts and local political authorities, retroactively apply new laws—these laws wouldn't come from legislation—they would be executive orders (not laws). They would be standards of executive fiat.

It would require a post-Constitutional order, even if the intention was to only suspend it temporarily, to get back to the Constitutional norms. No one in Washington is willing to do any of this.

To the extent that we are not honest with ourselves, to that extent American heritage will be gone in a few years. It is true that we are "losing our country." But we are losing it legally, within the permitted legal framework of the American system.

We would rather live the lie, remain in reputational good standing, live up to "our ideals," than save our country. Saving our country would imply all sorts of human, constitutional, financial, reputational casualties. It wouldn't just be uncomfortable like opposing the COVID regime;

there would be an onslaught of intense and gut wrenching guilt, a burden of carrying history on one's shoulders. None of these burdens are worth it. Our country and its heritage just isnt [sic] worth it.[105]

This is not a doom post. This is a face reality and do something about it post. This is a do what is required, and you can avoid the fate laid out post.[106]

Thomas Accord, a Christian teacher and author of *Who Is My Neighbor? An Anthology In Natural Relations* who was a panelist at Pastor Joel Webbon's 2025 Trashworld conference,[107] added this to the conversation:

I don't advocated [sic] deportations. They won't achieve the goal at which people are aiming. History and travel prove this.

What conservatives/MAGAs/rightists want will require bloodshed, violence, aggression, brutality

---

[105] Engel, C. (2025, September 5). *We are not being honest. If we want to reverse this stuff, technical mechanisms like deportations and remigration and immigration...* [Post]. X. https://x.com/contramordor/status/1963949895393345978

[106] Engel, C. (2025, September 5). *This is not a doom post. This is a face reality and do something about it post. This is a...* [Post]. X. https://x.com/contramordor/status/1964009529684660229

[107] Stevenson, B. (2025, May 5). So, I Went to See the Christian Nationalists... (Part 2). Letters to My Friends. https://bobstevenson.substack.com/p/so-i-went-to-see-the-christian-natio nalists-6a8

on mass scale. Not arrests, deportations, and paperwork. War.

A more ethnically and politically united U.S. in the 1800s tried to deport Africans but failed due to logistics, even though they had way more will and unity on the issue and way less people to deport than we do today.

We today have more tech/transportation means but not the hardened will and unity of mind to do the dirty deed. We are also dealing not with a few million powerless slaves but +55 million well-entrenched people. Basically several nations of peoples would need to be violently uprooted and brutally dispersed in a short period of time.

And you'd have to silence/combat liberals and their NGOs, politicians, academia, and especially their media organs due to all the ensuing pain, wailing, crimes, hatred, violence. You'd then need to ensure that those deported people, their descendants, their criminal/gang organizations, and their formal nations never ever ever retaliate against the U.S. or its citizens at home or abroad - for generations and generations.

Basically, what people are wanting today would require a blitz total war on +55 million people, followed by sustained imperial global power.[108]

Woke Right Identity Politics

Violent wolves who push both Woke Left and Woke Right ideologies commonly pretend to be Christians, use Christian language, and sometimes attempt to justify their positions using Bible verses taken out of context. But, like the original Communists who held to critical theories and participated in identity politics, there is nothing Christian about modern individuals who do these same things. Woke ideology, critical theories, and identity politics are evil because they rely on lies, they show partiality, and they commit injustice.

Those on the Woke Left and Woke Right will argue that an entire class of people (e.g., Whites, Pakistanis, or females) can be presumed to be on or against your side based

---

[108] Achord, T. (2025, September 5). *I don't advocated deportations. They won't achieve the goal at which people are aiming. History and travel prove this. What...* [Post]. X. https://x.com/ThomasAchord/status/1964086502880694524

on some characteristic that does not inherently make individuals in this class of people on your side or against your side. For instance, a woman who grew up in Pakistan and dresses like a Pakistani cannot be assumed to be anti-Right, anti-Christian, anti-Patriotic, and anti-American simply because of the way that she looks. It is possible for her to be a Christian, right-wing, patriotic American. Likewise, a White man who dresses sharply, has a family, and whose ancestors have been in America for over two-hundred years cannot be assumed to be pro-Christianity, pro-America, or pro-life. Even with these demographics, there is about a fifty-fifty chance that he is a secular, anti-Christian, pro-socialism, pro-choice liberal.

So, not only are identity politics moronic because they make assumptions like this, but it causes the adherents of Woke ideologies to believe lies about individual image bearers of God based on the class of people that they belong to. These lies are sinful, because they result in Woke adherents bearing false witness against their neighbors, which is forbidden by Exodus 20:16. Based on these lies, Woke adherents show favorable or unfavorable partiality towards entire classes of people, which is condemned by James 2:9 and Deuteronomy 1:17.

Although members of the Woke Left and Woke Right show partiality based on many different classes of people, the classes which they usually consider to be the most important (at this time in America) are race and ethnicity. This partiality can occur in small ways (e.g., by being rude to one class of people and kind to another class of people for no reason other than believing Woke lies about these groups) or very big ways (e.g., by advocating to deport or genocide an entire unfavored class of people and give their stuff to a favored class of people). If a government, in particular, shows partiality to entire classes of people for no reason other than their class, this will always result in injustice, which is strictly prohibited by God (Leviticus 19:15).

When confronted with this indictment, Woke Right wolves are apt to quote a single line, taken out of context, from the following passage, Titus 1:10-14:

> "For there are many rebellious men, empty talkers and deceivers, especially those of the circumcision, who must be silenced because they are upsetting whole families, teaching things they should not teach

for the sake of sordid gain. One of themselves, a prophet of their own, said, "Cretans are always liars, evil beasts, lazy gluttons." This testimony is true. For this reason reprove them severely so that they may be sound in the faith, not paying attention to Jewish myths and commandments of men who turn away from the truth.

They will say, if Paul could categorize an entire class of people as being liars, evil beasts, and lazy gluttons, then why can't we? Admittedly, this does sound like what Paul is saying, but only if you rip verses 12 and 13 out of their context, as quoted above in the full passage. In context, Paul is merely quoting a Cretan prophet to mock the Cretans in Titus' congregation who were among the *many* individuals who were rebellious, empty talkers who were upsetting whole families for sordid gain. Paul was not seriously saying that *all* Cretans were liars, evil beasts, and lazy gluttons. The very fact that Paul's complaint was with the "many" described at the beginning of the passage indicates that there were at least some who did not walk in these ways.

Since this Scripture does not prove their point, how do Woke Right wolves go about making their case? They fall back on the previously-mentioned concept of race-realism, an extra-Biblical pseudoscience that borrows much from Darwin's Theory of Evolution. There are many different variations of how race realism is alleged to work, but the primary proposal of the theory is that certain races are not only genetically superior or inferior compared to others, but also morally superior or inferior.

In Pastor Joel Webbon's podcast, *Yes, The Gospel Changes Genetics*, he and his co-host Wesley Todd advocated for the following view: those who are faithful to God will be rewarded with better, healthier, superior genetics. This includes oxytocin levels. Higher oxytocin levels improve "pair bonding," which helps couples stay married, helps men to not abandon their homes, and helps women raise their children better. This results in more moral societies, which then results in better genetics (causing a positive feedback loop). So, having better genetics (which is a reward from God for generational faithfulness to him) directly correlates to one racial group being more moral than another racial group.

It was pointed out on the podcast that East Asians have the highest oxytocin levels. This is perplexing for

Webbon's theory, since most East Asian societies have never been largely Christian and have not been "generationally faithful to God" like the Europeans have been. Americans have the second lowest levels of oxytocin of any people group, which Webbon stated is "because of our greatest strenth—diversity."[109]

Perhaps the greatest weakness of this theory, aside from the fact that it is a repackaged form of the heretical prosperity gospel applied to genetics, is the issue of women's oxytocin levels. Studies have shown that women have higher oxytocin levels than men.[110] Using Webbon's logic, this means that women have generationally been more faithful to God than men. What then should be done about this fact? If all women are more faithful to God then men, should men lose their right to vote? After all, they are not as righteous—and therefore not as fit to govern—as women. If we are not going to do anything with this fact—if we are not going to treat men and women differently because of differences in the physical and moral superiority of their

---

[109] Right Response Ministries. (2025, February 19). *Yes, the Gospel Changes Genetics* [Video]. YouTube. https://www.youtube.com/live/X6DamHcx8t8

[110] Owens, A. (2021, September 23). Tell Me All I Need to Know About Oxytocin. Health Central. https://www.healthcentral.com/mental-health/oxytocin

genetics—then why are we even bringing it up in the first place? Why would you say genetic differences matter and can be employed to save America, but not carry the argument out to the logical end by taking away votes from men and giving them to women, who have superior genetics to men?

Towards the end of this podcast, Webbon was asked, "Do you think the renewing of the mind by the gospel does fully overcome a genetic intelligence deficiency built up for generations of unbelief?" Webbon answered the question by saying,

> Significantly... I'm inclined to think fully. [...] But here's the caveat I would add: over generations. So no, I don't think that you can come from a people who for a thousand years were sexually not monogamous, using substance abuse [sic] and worshipping demons, violent, promiscuous, no system of sanitation, your diet is, instead of eating cows and cooking them, you use cow dung, you know, in your diet, I don't think you can come from that being your ancestry and then in five years, you know, or even twenty years, in one generation in your

personal life fully [...] overcome all of the genetic deficiencies and how that might affect things like intelligence or whatever all in the course of one generation. [...] That's my position, and if that's racist, then we just all need to admit that the word just doesn't mean anything. If that's how you define racism, then racism really isn't a sin.[111]

This question Webbon was asked appears to be in reference to Romans 12:2, which urges, "And do not be conformed to this world, but be transformed by the renewing of your mind, so that you may prove what the will of God is, that which is good and acceptable and perfect." Like all growth and sanctification that occurs in our lives, the renewal of the mind is a process which is accomplished by the power of God. We cannot take credit for any of this growth in our lives because it is God, and God alone, who gives the growth by His power (1 Corinthians 3:6).

To the extent anyone's mind can be "fully" renewed in this life, it is insane to deny that God has the power to make this change in a person's lifetime if that person has

---

[111] Right Response Ministries. (2025, February 19). *Yes, the Gospel Changes Genetics* [Video]. YouTube. https://www.youtube.com/live/X6DamHcx8t8

"inferior" genetics. The Holy Spirit is all-powerful and can renew anyone's mind as much as anyone else's. To deny that He has this power is pure, unadulterated, Satanic heresy, born out of sinful partiality and lies. As Matthew 19:26 promises, "With people this is impossible, but with God all things are possible."

Members of the Woke Right have a very short memory. Just a few years ago, many of them were rightly complaining about statements made by the Woke Left like the following: "*All* White people are colonizers and oppressors at heart. They are *all* proud and narcissistic and, because of that, *no* White person can ever be trusted." The Woke Left would then, inevitably (like all people who believe such things), use these lies about the White race to justify doing evil things to White people, such as prohibiting White people from being promoted at work; not giving an equal voice to White people; and advocating for requiring all White people to pay reparations.

When a White person hears the claims made by Woke Leftists about White people, he is right in concluding that they are lies because he, and many White people that he knows, are not like that. In the same way, when members of the Woke Right say that *all* Jews are parasites, they are lying. There are many hardworking Jews and lies like this are almost always used by the Woke Right to justify their desire to remove Jews from society. If the Woke Left should be condemned for playing identity politics, then so should the Woke Right.

Someone on the Woke Right might try to further defend himself by claiming, "Well, I'm not saying *all* Jews are thieves, but many of them are." What is the point of saying this then? Many White people are thieves too. In fact, there are many thieves in every race and ethnicity of people. "What I'm actually saying is that more Jews, as a percentage, are thieves than White people." Even if you could prove such a statement with hard statistics, what good would it do? We have already established that not *all* Jews are thieves, so neither you nor the government can take action against *all* of the Jews or treat them differently because of this.

In the same way, even though men are more likely to commit assault and homicide than women, we can't treat *all* men as if they are murderers. Or, even though White men are disproportionately the most likely demographic group to molest children,[112] which arguably is the most perverted, sick, and heinous of sins, we cannot treat *all* White men as though they are child molesters. Additionally, the vast majority of bestiality offenses[113] and mass shootings[114] are committed by White males. What action should be taken against White men in general because of this fact? If nothing should be done, then what is the point of even bringing up any of these facts in the first place? Why not just take action against all thieves, murderers, child molesters, mass shooters, and those who have sex with animals regardless of what race, ethnicity, or gender they are and leave it at that? Anything more than this requires practicing deceit and partiality.

---

[112] West, J. & Templer, D. (1994). Child molestation, rape, and ethnicity. NIH. https://pubmed.ncbi.nlm.nih.gov/7892399/

[113] Emmett, Lisa; Kasacek, Nina; and Stetina, Birgit Ursula (2021) "Demographic Characteristics of Individuals Who Abuse Animals: A Systematic Review," *People and Animals: The International Journal of Research and Practice:* Vol. 4 : Iss. 1, Article 3, pg. 23. https://docs.lib.purdue.edu/cgi/viewcontent.cgi?article=1070&context=pa ij

[114] Number of mass shootings in the United States between 1982 and August 2025, by shooter's race or ethnicity. (n.d.). Statista. Accessed September 14, 2025 from https://www.statista.com/statistics/476456/mass-shootings-in-the-us-by-shooter-s-race/

Rampant Reviling, Violent Threats, and Filthy Speech

Another major problem common to both the Woke Left and the Woke Right is rampant reviling. A reviler (the term used in the Bible) is someone who we would more commonly know today as a "verbal abuser" (someone who directs slander, foul language, or angry outbursts at others). The reason why this is a ubiquitous phenomenon in both the Woke Left and Woke Right is because neither of these movements have any good arguments. Their positions cannot withstand even small amounts of serious scrutiny, so they resort to angry torrents of name-calling and slandering their opponents as "gay" or "liberals" or "trannies" or "commies who hate America" or "motherfuckers" or "fascists."

They will respond to excellent objections from their opponents by telling them nothing more than to "get a life" or "fuck off" or, if they are talking to a woman, "go home and speak truth to your children" or "you're dressed like a slut and you need to dress more modestly." Since it is not possible for them to substantively engage with the arguments of their opponents, all that they can respond with is slander, angry cuss-words, and ad-hominems.

Not only do the followers of Woke wolves revile others, but it is common for the wolves to be revilers themselves. However, even the wolves who are not revilers are characterized by unwillingness to call out this sin in their followers. This is very dangerous for the souls of revilers, because Paul says those who live an unrepentant lifestyle of reviling will not inherit the kingdom of God (1 Corinthians 6:9). As Christians, we are sternly warned not to associate or even have a meal with anyone who claims to be a Christian but who is a reviler (1 Corinthians 5:11).

On top of this, wolves on the Woke Left and the Woke Right are oftentimes, but not always, known for their threats and filthy, vile speech. Matt Evans, a right-wing influencer who goes by "Beardson Beardly" online and is considered by the Groyper movement (a far-right network of internet activists primarily led by Nick Fuentes) to be Fuentes' "general,"[115] said the following to YouTuber Brittany Venti:

> Brittany, if I ever see you, I'm gonna rape you, in
> person... and I'm married. I'm going to fucking put

---

[115] Mangan, L. (2022, February 13). Louis Theroux's Forbidden America review – a terrifying meeting with the new far right. The Guardian. https://www.theguardian.com/tv-and-radio/2022/feb/13/louis-therouxs-forbidden-america-review-a-terrifying-meeting-with-the-new-far-right

my dick in your fucking asshole. Even if you've never had anal sex. Like, I'm going to hold you down, I'm gonna grab you by the back of your head, no lube, and I'm going to remove your pants, and I'm going to remove my pants and I'm going to stick my dick in your ass and I'm gonna rape you. Because you're such a dumb fucking bitch. That you do not understand... you have involved yourself into a community that you do not understand. And for that you're going to get anally raped.[116]

Elijah Schaffer, a right-wing influencer with more than 800,000 followers, had this to say on a show that he did with Pastor Joel Webbon:

I hate what women have become and I do hate it when women expect men in society to uphold the natural masculine tendencies. Women are literally going after the top 10 percent of men, which are what kind of men: I saw a tweet that said, "It's crazy that in 2025 to pull bitches, you literally have to be like a millionaire, 6'7, drive a Lamborghini, and be White."

---

[116] Cassie Schindler Baked Alaska Anthime Gionet Vids. (2022, February 18). *'Beardson Beardly' (Matt Evans) rape threat to Brittany Venti [Nick Fuentes AFPAC Forbidden America]* [Video]. YouTube. https://www.youtube.com/watch?v=mzq8vzr18ao

So women are still going after men that emulate the most masculine tendencies, right? They're going for tall, rich, famous men. And men, what do we get? The women, they're just whores. They can't even cook a Hot Pocket.

That's why once you have sex with them, once you cum, you come to your senses. You have that post-ejaculate clarity—post-nut clarity, they call it on online these days—but you realize after you nut, you're like you're just a bunch of holes. And that's really sad because it devalues women, so then your view of women becomes so low because women really are just a bunch of holes today. But that doesn't mean that's who they have to be or who God made them to be or what they should be. And I think that a lot of the hatred that I have towards women, and a lot of the hatred a lot of men have towards women, is simply the product of generations of sin and rebellion that have created women to be something that they're not.[117]

---

[117] Mantyla, K. (2025, August 27). 'Just A Bunch Of Holes': Elijah Schaffer And Joel Webbon Share Their Thoughts On Women. People for the American Way.

Although Pastor Webbon sat silently through this rant, he joined in the filthy conversation at another point in the show:

"...Things have changed. I've had to travel around the world and meet with very, very weird people and cool people to try to make this stuff happen. And, unlike Sorbo over here, my knees were not bruised and hurt through those meetings," Schaffer commented.

"You've gotta get ahead somehow," Braeden Sorbo interjected.

Schaffer replied, "Well it was 'ahead' not 'get head,' not 'give head.' 'Get ahead,' not give it."

Pastor Webbon then added, "But not if you're Kevin Sorbo's son. You don't have to do that! Elijah might, but not you. You're good. You're good to go!"[118]

It is completely unseemly for people who call themselves Christians, let alone someone who calls himself a Christian pastor, to engage in such disgusting, crude joking.

---

https://www.peoplefor.org/rightwingwatch/just-bunch-holes-elijah-schaffer-and-joel-webbon-share-their-thoughts-women

[118] Hilaire Nereus. (2025, August 26). *Joel Webbon, Pastor of Covenant Bible Church in Georgetown, making jokes about men giving oral sex to other men in...* [Post with video of Elijah Schaffer's show]. X. https://x.com/HilaireNereus/status/1960434783328329865

Ephesians 4:29 states, "Let no unwholesome word proceed from your mouth, but only such a word as is good for edification according to the need of the moment, so that it will give grace to those who hear." Similarly, Ephesians 5:3-4 commands, "But immorality or any impurity or greed must not even be named among you, as is proper among saints; and there must be no filthiness and silly talk, or coarse jesting, which are not fitting, but rather giving of thanks." If these admonitions have any application at all, they certainly forbid this type of smutty, indecent conversation participated in by Schaffer and Pastor Webbon.

Such conversations are not Christian at all, but are deeply pagan. While this is just an example, those who are familiar with the Woke Left and Woke Right know that this type of speech is highly pervasive among these groups; this makes sense, since there is nothing truly Christian about either of these groups. Rather, they are pagan. They often believe the same thing pagans do, act like pagans, and talk like pagans. As our Lord said in Luke 6:45,

> The good man out of the good treasure of his heart
> brings forth what is good; and the evil man out of the

evil treasure brings forth what is evil; for his mouth speaks from that which fills his heart.

Totalitarianism

The end goal of Woke Left and Woke Right ideologies, as well as critical theories and identity politics in general, is always totalitarianism. The end game of the American Woke Left is to establish a Communist utopia where the state has total power and forces society into an atheistic communal "utopia." The final goal of the American Woke Right is to establish a nominally-Christian kingdom where the church and state are completely integrated and which will be ruled by an all-powerful and perfect "Christian Prince" who will promote the interests of all "Heritage" Americans by putting Blacks, Jews, and women back in their rightful place.

Historically, totalitarian governments have almost always sought to expand their rule by conquering other nations. The Communist utopia of the Woke Left will invade other nations to bring the utopia to them as well, with the end goal of becoming a global empire. Likewise, the Christian Prince in America will choose to bring the unified

"Christian" government and church to less fortunate nations and will expand his empire over the whole world.

This is the ultimate vision of Dominionists, who believe that the church will take dominion over the whole world *before* Christ returns. This position has been labelled by some as "eschatological feminism," since it believes that the church (the Bride) will go out and do all of the work and conquering which Christ (the Husband) is supposed to do. This is ironic, considering that many Dominionists are patriarchal and anti-feminist in all matters except this one. Those who argue for this position are arguing for the Bride to get victory and glory from her earthly accomplishments which rightfully belong to the Husband alone. But irony aside, this worldview is false. When Christ returns, He will conquer all the nations of the world Himself and get the victory and glory (Revelation 19 and 20).

The totalitarianism promoted by the Woke Right and Woke Left is an evil thing which makes idols out of the state and human princes and is condemned by God (Psalm 146:3-4). When the people of Israel came to Samuel and demanded a king, God said in 1 Samuel 8:7-8,

> Listen to the voice of the people in regard to all that they say to you, for they have not rejected you, but they have rejected Me from being king over them. Like all the deeds which they have done since the day that I brought them up from Egypt even to this day—in that they have forsaken Me and served other gods—so they are doing to you also.

Because the Israelites desired to have an all-powerful king like the pagan nations that surrounded them, in 1 Samuel 8:11-18, God warned what would happen to them when they got what they wished for. God's warning here is is something that all Woke Left and Woke Right wolves who long for a totalitarian government that will crush their enemies should take to heart:

> This will be the procedure of the king who will reign over you: he will take your sons and place them for himself in his chariots and among his horsemen and they will run before his chariots. He will appoint for himself commanders of thousands and of fifties, and some to do his plowing and to reap his harvest and to make his weapons of war and equipment for his chariots. He will also take your daughters for

perfumers and cooks and bakers. He will take the best of your fields and your vineyards and your olive groves and give them to his servants. He will take a tenth of your seed and of your vineyards and give to his officers and to his servants. He will also take your male servants and your female servants and your best young men and your donkeys and use them for his work. He will take a tenth of your flocks, and you yourselves will become his servants. Then you will cry out in that day because of your king whom you have chosen for yourselves, but the LORD will not answer you in that day.

To get vengeance on their enemies and gain absolute totalitarian power, members of the Woke Left and Woke Right will stop at nothing. Nothing is too extreme for them if it results in them getting or staying in power. As Corey Mahler was quoted in the beginning of this book, "Genocide is a legitimate tool of statecraft, and the Christian prince may employ it when warranted."[119]

---

[119] Curcio, L. (2024, September 4). *Genocide is a legitimate tool of statecraft, and the Christian prince may employ it when warranted...* [Image showing a post made by Corey Mahler, containing the previous quote]. X. https://x.com/MethodMinistry/status/1831496005512261801

Wokeness in the End Times

In 2 Timothy 1:1-9, Paul wrote about the type of people who will dominate the world in the end times, a description which seems to perfectly describe the character of those on the Woke Left and Woke Right:

> But realize this, that in the last days difficult times will come. For men will be lovers of self, lovers of money, boastful, arrogant, revilers, disobedient to parents, ungrateful, unholy, unloving, irreconcilable, malicious gossips, without self-control, brutal, haters of good, treacherous, reckless, conceited, lovers of pleasure rather than lovers of God, holding to a form of godliness, although they have denied its power; avoid such men as these. For among them are those who enter into households and captivate weak women weighed down with sins, led on by various impulses, always learning and never able to come to the knowledge of the truth. Just as Jannes and Jambres opposed Moses, so these men also oppose the truth, men of depraved mind, rejected in regard to the faith. But they will not make further progress; for

their folly will be obvious to all, just as Jannes's and Jambres's folly was also.

Today, arrogant Woke Right boasters are running around in the church unironically saying, "I'm one of the best we've got!" Revilers call godly brothers and sisters who disagree with them "gay retards" five times a day. Wolves disrespect their parents and church fathers by dismissively saying things like, "Okay, Boomer," and, "May God rescue you from your Boomer brain." Many of those on the Woke Left and Woke Right, including their pastors, have no self-control, evidenced by their inability to go a single day without reviling someone on social media.

Brutal Woke Leftists in South Africa advocate for killing all White farmers and brutal "Christian" wolves on the Woke Right in America propose shooting and killing immigrants who try to cross the border, even if they are Christian women or children, "to make an example out of them." Reckless Woke Leftists in America burn down entire cities when a court case doesn't go their way.

Many of these individuals, on both the Woke Left and Woke Right, hold to a form of godliness, trying to appear as though they are godly Christians. In the case of the Woke

Left, this is done by singing modern worship songs, getting "Jesus is my anchor" tattoos, and adding Micah 6:8 bumper stickers to their cars. In the case of the Woke Right, this is done by raising big families, singing old hymns, going to "Trashworld" conferences, making sourdough bread, and starting anonymous X accounts to wage holy war against the infidels. Although there is nothing inherently wrong with these extrinsics, they are powerless to save anyone.

Members of the Woke Right and Woke Left who have these characteristics (brutality, reviling, recklessness, conceit, etc.) described by Paul are not saved; they have never accepted God's mercy and lovingkindness in their hearts or received the true power needed from Him to change their lives. Instead of acknowledging this and yielding to God's sweet forgiveness, they proceed from bad to worse and become wolves who pray on the weak, gullible, and those who are already laden with sins, thus making even more disciples of Hell.

Brothers and sisters, based on this passage (with its amazing prophetic foresight) and the rise of the Woke Right and Woke Left around the world, we must be getting closer and closer to the end times. It is disturbing to consider that these groups will only get worse and worse before the end of the Tribulation. C.S. Lewis also foresaw this development beginning in his lifetime:

> Fascism and Communism, like all other evils, are potent because of the good they contain or imitate. *Diabolus simius Dei* [the devil is the ape of God]. And, of course, their occasion is the failure of those who left humanity starved of that particular good.
>
> This does not for me alter the conviction that they are very bad indeed. One of the things we must guard against is the penetration of both into Christianity—availing themselves of that very truth you have suggested and I have admitted.
>
> Mark my words: you will presently see both a Leftist and a Rightist pseudo-theology developing – the abomination will stand where it ought not.[120]

Indeed, even our Lord prophesied of distressing days to come as we approach the end of this age, when he warned, "Because lawlessness is increased, most people's love will grow cold." As we get closer and closer to the return of Christ, wicked lawlessness will proliferate across the world.

---

[120] Stroud, R. (2022, April 9). C.S. Lewis & Karl Marx. Mere Inkling Press. https://mereinkling.net/tag/marxism/

The primary temptation that we face when we see this lawlessness is to become tribal, remove love from our hearts, and become brutal towards our enemies. Leftists have brought great evil on society, causing the love of many on the Right to grow cold. As we are seeing, the Right is becoming increasingly bloodthirsty and barbaric towards those on the Left, even being willing to forsake all of their deepest-held beliefs and principles to destroy their enemies. This will cause the Left to become even more wicked in response to the evil of the Right. This is a vicious cycle which Christians must not get caught up in for the sake of our souls.

Until Christ returns, Exodus 23:2 has an important warning for Christians: "You shall not follow the masses in doing evil, nor shall you testify in a dispute so as to turn aside after a multitude in order to pervert justice." Do not follow the Woke Left or Woke Right masses into their ever-increasing, genocidal evils. When the Woke Left or Woke Right mobs come after you and demand that you bend the truth to fit their narratives, do not cave to them, regardless of whether or not they are on "your team." Call out the wolves and preach repentance to their followers. Be strong and let the following verse from Paul (Galatians 1:10) be your motto when you are confronting them: "For am I now seeking the favor of men, or of God? Or am I striving to please men? If I were still trying to please men, I would not be a bond-servant of Christ."

The Swastika in the Sanctuary

Chapter IV: Anti-Jewish and Anti-Israelite Partiality

A key tenet of Nazi doctrine, and one of its greatest heresies, is the partiality and Satanic hatred that it shows towards Jews and Israelites. This truth has been recognized by real Christians ever since the inception of Nazism. In 1933, soon after Hitler became Chancellor of Germany, C.S. Lewis wrote the following:

> [...] Nothing can fully excuse the iniquity of Hitler's persecution of the Jews, or the absurdity of his theoretical position. Did you see that he said "The Jews have made no contribution to human culture and in crushing them I am doing the will of the Lord." Now as the whole idea of the "Will of the Lord" is precisely what the world owes to the Jews, the blaspheming tyrant has just fixed his absurdity for all to see in a single sentence, and shown that he is as contemptible for his stupidity as he is detestable for his cruelty. For the German people as a whole we ought to have charity: but for dictators, "Nordic"

tyrants and so on – well, read the chapter about Mr Savage in the *Regress* and you have my views.[121]

Anti-Jewish partiality certainly did not originate with the Nazis. Such attitudes are endemic in European paganism, Islam, Communism, and many other political ideologies and false religions. To learn more about the fascinating topic of Jewish persecution in the Soviet Union, since people who are ignorant of history often assert without evidence that Communism is Jewish, I highly recommend reading the fascinating book *Out Of The Red Shadows: Anti-Semitism in Stalin's Russia* by Gennadi Kostyrchenko. Sadly, the Christian church has not been exempt from committing the sin of anti-Jewish partiality as well.

The History of Anti-Jewish Partiality in the Church

The church's struggle with this sin goes back far in its history to when the original Jewish apostles and believers died out and Gentiles began to outnumber Jews in the church and hold the majority of leadership roles. This sin became a key feature of the Catholic church and even continued to be practiced by many Protestants during and after the

---

[121] Politics in C. S. Lewis's Collected Letters. (2024). Lewisiana. https://www.lewisiana.nl/politics/

Reformation. Why did this happen? Satan is filled with jealousy and hatred for the Israelite people, who God sovereignly chose (Romans 11:28); bestowed His *unmerited* favor on, no matter how much they stray from Him and into sin (the book of Hosea is all about this); and made an eternal, irrevocable covenant with, which will last as long as the universe itself (Jeremiah 31:35-36). As nominal Christianity became the dominant religion among the Gentile world powers in the West, Satan (who is the god of this world, according to 2 Corinthians 4:4) used his control over the false church and "Christian" magistrates to carry out his evil, murderous schemes regarding the Israelites.

Satan was able to accomplish this because of the rampant allegorization of Scripture popularized by the Catholic church; the invention of new teachings like replacement theology (also known as supersessionism, the belief that the church either *is* Israel or has replaced or superseded Israel, with all of Israel's Old Testament promises interpreted to apply only to the church, but not any of Israel's curses, in a stunning display of inconsistent hermeneutics); and the inaccessibility of the Bible to the common man. As long as the Catholic and Orthodox churches taught absurd allegorical interpretations of the Bible and kept the Word of God from laypersons, deceiving Christians to hate and persecute the Jews was easy for the god of this age. For example, in Numbers 24:9, referring to Israel, Balaam prophesied, "Blessed is everyone who blesses you, and cursed is everyone who curses you." When this verse was either kept from the common man or allegorized to refer to the church, removing the prophecy from its original context, it was easy for Christians to feel that they were at liberty to curse and harm Israel.

After the Protestant Reformation, the Bible became more and more accessible to normal Christians, who started to read it for themselves and realize they had been taught lies their whole lives. A growing minority of Protestant Christians, in particular, began to believe that God still had a plan for Israel and that the church should not behave arrogantly towards the modern-day Israelites as the Apostle Paul commanded, even if they are enemies of the church (Romans 11:18 and 11:28). This gave rise to groups of Christians, like the Puritans, who predominantly held to historic premillennialism, the belief that Jesus will return before the Millennial Reign, as indicated by Revelation 19 and 20. These groups also believed that the nation of Israel would be returned to its ancient land and be saved when Christ returned (Romans 11:25-26). In so doing, they returned to the beliefs held by the earliest church fathers, who, having been discipled by the authors of the Bible, also unanimously held to the doctrine of historic premillennialism[122] and the future salvation of the Jews.[123]

A number of Christians throughout church history, although they were in the minority, have always held to Biblical views about the future salvation of the Jews. Their belief stems from a straightforward interpretation of Romans 11, which is compatible with a wide range of theological views. For evidence of this claim, see Doug Wilson's *Boast Not Against the Branches: The Reformed Tradition and the Jews* or Marsh and Fazio's, *Discovering Dispensationalism: Tracing the Development of Dispensational Thought From the First to the Twenty-First Century*. As corrupt Catholic teachings continued to be reformed and wrestled out of Protestant churches, Dispensationalism (the belief that God

---

[122] Gibbon, E. (1993). *The Decline and Fall of the Roman Empire*. Vol. I. Pp. 514-515. Alfred A. Knopf, a division of Penguin Random House LLC. (Original work published in 1776).
[123] Vlach, M. (2015, May 20). Church History and Israel's Future. The Master's Seminary.
https://blog.tms.edu/church_history_and_israels_future

has interacted with humanity, including Israel and the church, in rigidly distinct ways throughout history) arose in the 1800s and became popular in English speaking nations, especially Britain and America. More recently, Progressive Dispensationalism developed, which is similar to classic Dispensationalism, but less rigid, acknowledging that God works with the church, Israel, and every other nation at the same time and bestows promises on these distinct entities which are shared mutually and cumulate through history, a view which you can learn more about in Blaising and Block's excellent book, *Progressive Dispensationalism.*

These theological systems have helped give the church the most Biblically-accurate understanding of the relationship between the church and the people of Israel that it has had since the first century, helping to heal the divide between these two branches on the tree of God's redemptive plan. But, thanks to the Woke Left and the Woke Right, anti-Jewish partiality—in all of its Satanic ugliness—has been attempting to take over the church again. Although different denominations view the Jewish people differently, anti-Jewish partiality is unnecessary under any of the major orthodox theological positions and should never be practiced because of the commands and promises found in Romans 11.

What is Anti-Jewish Partiality?

Why am I using the term "anti-Jewish partiality" and "anti-Israelite partiality" instead of "antisemitism" or "anti-Jewish racism?" People who hate the Jews (and those who are sympathetic to people who hate the Jews) are fond of pointing out that the words "racism" and "antisemitism" do not exist in the Bible. Since they can't find these words in the Bible, they conclude that there is nothing inherently wrong or sinful about racism or antisemitism (some even call these sins "fake sins").

This objection is as idiotic as it is childish. Pedophilia-supporters could also point out that the word "pedophilia" never appears in the Bible and, therefore, Christians who say that pedophilia is wrong are being Pharisees. However, the Bible says that children and young teenagers do not know the difference between right and wrong (Deuteronomy 1:39) and, if they do not even know this difference, how could they possibly consent to sex? Additionally, the Bible *only* uses Greek and Hebrew terms for adult men and women to refer to husbands and wives (by contrast, Jesus referred to a twelve year old girl as still being a little girl, in Mark 5:41-42). Through inference, this clearly means that all sexual relations with a child or young teenager are prohibited in Christianity, since the only lawful sexual relationships are those which occur in marriage and only adults can be married, according to the Bible. But, since the word "pedophilia" does not specifically appear in the Bible, the pedophilia-supporter will ignore all of these arguments and will proclaim that pedophilia is a "fake sin."

Likewise, there are stories about sinful racism in the Bible (Numbers 12:1 and Galatians 2:11-12) and it is obvious that racism and antisemitism are the sins of partiality (James 2:9), but since the exact words "racism" and "antisemitism" don't appear in the Bible, they must be "fake sins." Because of moronic objections like this, I chose to describe the sins of antisemitism and racism against the Jews as "anti-Jewish partiality" in this section. In an ideal world, where everyone is an adult and refrains from using childish arguments, it would not be necessary for me to use terms like these. Even though it is obvious why racism and antisemitism are sins, the Woke Right speech police have forced us to dumb things down for them.

Without a doubt, partiality is a sin in Christianity (Exodus 23:2-3, Leviticus 19:15, Deuteronomy 1:17, 2 Chronicles 19:6-7, Proverbs 24:23, and James 2:9). Anti-Jewish partiality, specifically, can take one of four different forms. First, it can be expressed as partiality against the Jewish race. This occurs when a Jew's perceived physiognomy or racial characteristics are observed (e.g., having a large, hook nose; dark beady eyes; drooping eyelids; or red hair) and she is treated worse *because of her race*—she is assumed to be a Communist or a traitor; her business is boycotted; she is slandered, insulted, and mocked on the internet; or she is taken to a concentration camp.

Second, anti-Jewish partiality can be expressed as partiality against the Jewish ethnicity. This occurs when people treat Jews worse after observing elements of their ethnicity (e.g., star of David symbols, Jewish dress, Jewish music and dancing, Jewish food, etc.). This type of partiality occurs when someone sees a star of David on a Jewish school and vandalizes it by spray-painting a swastika over it. Another example would be someone who sees a man wearing traditional Jewish clothing (i.e., a black hat and black suit) and proceeds to beat him up, take his stuff, deny him business, or force him to wear an armband with a yellow star.

Many wolves who have rampant anti-Jewish partiality in their hearts are smart enough to know that they cannot vocalize their partiality against the Jews because of their race or ethnicity while pretending to be Christians; too many Christians today would see past this and refuse to support their "ministries," causing the wolves to lose a lot of money, which, along with fame, is the thing they care most about in life. So their reasoning for being partial against the Jews is oftentimes ostensibly because of the next two reasons.

The third type of anti-Jewish partiality is attributed to being anti-Zionist or anti-Israel. *Zionism* is the belief that the Israelites should establish and defend a nation-state in the ancient land of Israel. There are passages in the Bible which prophecy about the return of the nation of Israel *a second time* from a diaspora to its land *never to be uprooted again* (Isaiah 11:11, Ezekiel 36-37, and Amos 9:14-15) and indicate that Israel will be given even more land in the future, likely during the Millennial Reign (Genesis 15:18-21). The first regathering to the land of Israel occurred after the Tribe of Judah's return from the Babylonian Exile, and the second is in the process of unfolding today, two thousand years after the Roman Exile. Although Zionism can be supported by the Bible, it is not necessary to believe the Bible or even be religious to support the idea that modern-day Israel should be able to maintain and defend their nation-state, which is all that Zionism strictly entails.

Since this is the claim of Zionism, those who are *anti-Zionist* believe that the people of Israel should *not* have a right to maintain and defend their nation. Thus, those who are anti-Zionist are also anti-Israel. This makes anti-Zionism an expressly genocidal belief, since it argues that the people of Israel should be removed from their homes and their land. During the process of this forcible removal, what will happen to the Jews who inevitably choose to put up an armed resistance and defend their homes? Morally, they have a right to defend their homes (Nehemiah 4:14). Will they be killed en masse for doing what they have the moral right to do? If so, anti-Zionism, as an ideology, not only expresses the desire to steal land and property from millions of people which is evil enough, but it is also outright murderous in its plan to kill all those who resist.

Clearly, being anti-Zionist or anti-Israel shows partiality against the people of Israel who reside in the modern-day state of Israel, which includes many Christians. If you strive to see an entire nation of innocent civilians removed from their land and homes where they have lived their whole lives, then you are acting with partiality against these Israelites.

The three forms of Anti-Israelite partiality discussed so far can occur irrespective of religion. Many people who are partial against the Jews for these three reasons would not care if the Jew was a Christian. They would gladly be partial against Messianic Jews because of their race, ethnicity, home in Israel, or support for the existence of Israel, even though they are followers of Christ.

The last form of anti-Jewish partiality that we will discuss is partiality against the Jews because of the religion of Judaism. Do not misunderstand me on this: it is acceptable for a Christian to be aware of the religious differences of others and to treat others differently based on their religious differences *in some Biblically-defined circumstances.* For example, 2 Corinthians 6:14 warns us to "not be bound together with unbelievers." So, a Christian may refuse to enter into a business venture with a non-believer (a Neo-Nazi, for example) for the sole reason that he is a non-believer.

However, when it comes to showing partiality against people by refusing to give them justice, lying about them, stealing their property, or murdering them on account of their religion (even if it is a false religion), it is strictly forbidden. Deuteronomy 1:17 says, "You shall not show partiality in judgment." It does not say, "You shall not show partiality in judgment, unless the individual practices a false religion. Then you may lie about him and pervert justice."

Adding more depth to this issue is the fact that Judaism is only a false religion if a practicing Jew rejects the Messiah, as there are hundreds of thousands of Messianic Jews across the world. These are Christians who practice the Biblical religion of Judaism (for example, by wearing tzitzit, as described in Numbers 15:37–41 and Deuteronomy 22:12, or by observing Passover, which is spoken of in Exodus 12) and extra-biblical Jewish ethnic and religious observances (for instance, celebrating Hanukkah, which the Jews were never commanded to observe in the Torah or the Prophets). It is completely acceptable for Christians to practice Judaism in this way, since our God, *Yeshua Hamashiach* (Jesus the Messiah), and all of the Apostles practiced Judaism in this way too. Yeshua observed both the Biblical requirements of Judaism (e.g., by observing Passover, according to Matthew 26:17-30) and the extra-Biblical elements as well (e.g., his participation in Hanukkah, the Festival of Dedication, according to John 10:22-23). Similarly, long into the Apostle Paul's ministry and long *after* the Crucifixion of Jesus, Paul participated in ritual purity vows and sacrifices at the Temple to show that he was still keeping the Law of Moses and approved of the Jews doing this as well (Acts 21:17-26).

Thus, it cannot be said that Judaism, by itself, is deserving of any type of partiality against it. Those who make this claim would show partiality against their own Savior and God Himself, in addition to all of the Apostles. On top of this, even though many wolves say that they are "anti-Zionist" or are opposed to the Jewish religion as a cover, it is clear from other things that they say that they are anti-Jewish partialists in general. A person may claim that he is "anti-Zionist", but if he then proceeds to call all Jews "parasites," his hatred likely runs deeper than just "anti-Zionism".

In light of this evidence, claims like the following from Pastor Joel Webbon should be seen as the exceedingly wicked statements that they are:

> As a Christian pastor, providentially placed in America, my chief focus is to disciple American Christians. And one of the particular areas where American Christians need to be discipled is in recognizing that Jesus hates Judaism with a perfect hatred.[124]

Did Jesus hate the religion that He flawlessly practiced with perfect hatred? Should someone who claims to be a Christian hate the religion that his Messiah practiced with perfect hatred? If they had seen the Messiah and the Apostles celebrating Hanukkah or wearing tzitzit or making sacrifices at the Temple, would they have hated this with perfect hatred and used this hatred for Judaism as an excuse to show sinful partiality against Yeshua and the Apostles? Should Christians show partiality against Jews today for the

---

[124] Webbon, J. (2024, December 9). *1) Instructing Christians in America, who have undergone a thorough psyop for the last 80 years, that Judaism is a...* [Post]. X. https://x.com/rightresponsem/status/1866127952909320378

sole reason that they are doing things which Jesus and the Apostles did?

Even after Jesus Christ had completed His earthly mission, the Apostle Paul said in Romans 9:4-5 that a practicing Jew is one,

> to whom belongs [notice how this is present tense] the adoption as sons, and the glory and the covenants and the giving of the Law and the temple service and the promises, whose are the fathers, and from whom is the Christ according to the flesh, who is over all, God blessed forever. Amen.

Webbon also stated, "The most Jewish thing a person can do is reject Christ."[125] Similarly, Candace Owens, referring to a comment from someone pointing out that Christianity began with Messianic Jews, remarked, "And those Jews became Christian. Full stop. There is no hyphenated faith. You are either a Christian or you are a Jew."[126] Have these wolves not read Acts 22:3, where the Apostle Paul states plainly, "I am a Jew"? Paul had been a

---

[125] Webbon, J. (2025, August 31). *False. The most Jewish thing a person can do is reject Christ. Christ is King.* [Post]. X. https://x.com/rightresponsem/status/1962145563823985100

[126] Owens, C. (2025, August 29). *And those Jews became Christian. Full stop. There is no hyphenated faith. You are either a Christian or...* [Post]. X. https://x.com/RealCandaceO/status/1961438519319990310

Christian for a very long time when he said this. Or, what about John 4:22, where Yeshua is speaking to the Samaritan woman and, in context if you read John 4, refers to Himself as a Jew: "You worship what you do not know; we [Jews] worship what we know, for salvation is from the Jews." If salvation is from the Jews, how on earth is rejecting Christ the most Jewish thing a person can do? If Christ referred to Himself as a Jew, why would anyone say that you must be either a Christian or a Jew?

Clearly, there is nothing inherently wrong about the Jewish religion itself and, because of Bible verses like these, the term "Judeo-Christian" is a perfectly acceptable term to use in many contexts, since the Christian faith has its foundation with religious, racial, and ethnic Jews. It is impossible to even understand Christianity apart from its religious Jewish foundations, since Yeshua is the promised Jewish Messiah. Rather, when it comes to Judaism today, the only issue for *some* modern Jews who practice Judaism is that they are not Messianic Jews or—more plainly put—that they reject their Messiah. Not all Jews who practice Judaism reject the Messiah, since there are many Messianic Jews across the world.

Accordingly, it is sinful to practice partiality against a Jew solely because he practices the same Jewish religion that His Messiah practiced. If you show partiality by deporting, stealing from, beating up, harassing, excluding, or murdering a Jew who practices this type of Judaism, you would have done the same thing to your Messiah. However, it is not sinful to practice Biblically permissible types of partiality (e.g., not going into business together) against someone solely because he rejects Jesus as his Messiah, regardless of his race, ethnicity, or religion.

A potential objection to this would be the claim that Talmudic or Rabbinic Judaism is a false religion. This is somewhat true, although the problem is not with Judaism, for the reasons previously explained. The problem is with the Talmud, a collection of writings and debates between Rabbis over Scripture which includes many false teachings, some of which are abhorrent, and which frequently add and take away from the Law of God. The Rabbis who teach the Talmud effectively do the same sinful work that the Pharisees were doing in the days of Jesus, and those who follow the teachings of the Talmud and Talmudic Rabbis do so to their own detriment.

However, Christianity also has the same problem with false teachers, modern day Pharisees, who add and take away things from the Law and teach abhorrent things. For instance, some of these wicked men, like Joel Webbon, advocate for shooting and killing migrants at the border to make an example out of them,[127] an abhorrent thing which violates God's commands to not do violence to the foreigner (Jeremiah 22:3 and Zechariah 7:9-10). Additionally, some of these teachers of iniquity add to the Law by falsely claiming that God prohibits women from voting or serving in the government, a prohibition which does not exist anywhere in the Word of God and which clearly is not legitimate because of the example of Deborah (Judges 4-5). Since Christianity has a problem with some false teachers who add and subtract from the Law and teach abhorrent things, should Christianity be considered as a false religion? Should the baby be thrown out with the bathwater? No, certainly not. Rather, for both Christianity and Judaism, specific false teachings and false teachers should be condemned.

---

[127] Mantyla, K. (2024, November 14). 'They Need To Be Killed': Joel Webbon Says Anyone Trying To Cross The Border Must Be Shot. People for the American Way.
https://www.peoplefor.org/rightwingwatch/they-need-be-killed-joel-webbon-says-anyone-trying-cross-border-must-be-shot

Parasites

Even after providing all of this nuance, however, it is important to remember that almost all of those who claim they are only partial against the Jewish religion are actually partial against Jewish people instead and are merely using this excuse as a cover, if you pay close attention to the things that they say. I submit the following statement from Pastor Joel Webbon, which was previously quoted at the beginning of this book, to the analysis of the reader:

> Judaism by nature, in its ideology and its religion, is, I believe, parasitical. And, yes, I'm using the word parasitical. [...] Yes, parasitical. I'm not calling each and every Jew parasitical. I'm not saying that. I'm saying Judaism, as an ideology and as a religion, I do believe is parasitical—that what it has done historically, throughout the ages, is typically go into other countries, other peoples, with other religions, and kind of cozy up, but not really for their benefit. Not a mutually beneficial relationship, but where they ultimately get far more out of the deal than the Christian nation does. Judaism has thrived on Christendom. If Christendom falls and the West falls,

and Islam wins the day, Muslims will not play nice with Jews. They will be screwed. Jews need Christians. Christians do not need Jews. It is not a mutually beneficial relationship.[128]

How, exactly, does a religion sneak into Christian nations, "cozy up" to Christians, and leech off of them? This is not something that a religion magically does; it is something that people do. In this case, Webbon alleges that the Jewish people, in general, do this. It is apparent that the chief allegation is not that Judaism is parasitical, but that Jewish people are parasitical. If the complaint was really against Judaism, the complainant should have been able to point to a specific verse in the Old Testament or a specific writing in the Talmud which instructs Jews to be parasites. There are no teachings in either of these sources which instruct to Jews to be "parasites" or to sneak into Christian countries, "cozy up" to Christians, and extract benefits from them without providing anything in return.

If there is no evidence that Judaism "by nature" or in "its ideology" or "its religion" teaches Jews to be parasites,

---

[128] Unsupervised Woman Tweeting. (2024, December 2). "*Judaism, by nature, in its ideology and its religion is, I believe, parasitical. And yes, I'm using the word parasitical.*".... [Post with video]. X. https://x.com/HasBrainCanRead/status/1863642742481354851

then it is apparent that this complaint is not against Judaism, but against Jews. If someone says, "Christianity is a colonizing religion that takes over native peoples, steals from them, and rapes their women," this is not a complaint against Christianity, because Christianity does not teach any of these things. Rather, it is a complaint against Christians which contains false allegations, equally as false as the allegation that the industrious, creative Jewish people are parasites.

The Jews have provided much to the world in the fields of science (the Theory of Relativity, the Theory of Nuclear Energy, quantum mechanics, and biochemistry), technology (televisions, computers, gas-powered cars, cybernetics, microphones, helicopters, Google, packet switching and the internet, bullet proof glass, nuclear submarines, sewing machines, USB flash drives, ballpoint pens, automatic transmissions, mobile phones, and color photography), and medicine (typhoid tests, streptomycin, the discovery of blood types, vitamins, the insulin measurement method, defibrillators, and pregnancy tests) which we all benefit from. It is incredibly ironic for anyone who does not have a "real" job, but Tweets inflammatory things for a living, to drive to a recording studio in a gas-powered car (invented by Siegfried Marcus, a Jew) with an automatic transmission (invented by László Bíró, a Jew) and then use a computer (invented by Herman Goldstine, a Jew), a microphone (invented by Emile Berliner, a Jew), and the internet (made possible by packet switching, which was invented by Paul Baran, a Jew) to broadcast a video to YouTube (owned by Google, which was founded by Larry Page and Sergey Brin, who are Jews) which will primarily be streamed by an audience using mobile phones (invented by Martin Cooper, a Jew) to whine like a spoiled-rotten kid about how the Jews are parasites.

Another thing to notice is that, by the end of the quote from Webbon, Jews are explicitly being talked about. If the Jews that are mentioned at the end of the quote are the same Jews who practice the Judaism which somehow sneaks into Christian nations and "cozies up" to Christians, then these Jews are being called parasites. This appears to be a textbook example of how a person can claim to be decrying the religion of Judaism, when his animosity is actually directed towards the Jewish people in general.

Why is the Woke Right obsessed with calling the Jews "parasites?" Some of these influencers are merely stupid and repeat talking points they have heard without considering their origins or implications. But, for the wolves who are aware of what they are doing, they refer to the Jews as "parasites" for the same reason that many pro-choice advocates call babies in the womb "parasites." By calling an image bearer of God a "parasite," this helps a perpetrator dehumanize his victim and carry out some horrible action against her (e.g., murder and theft). That is exactly why Adolf Hitler wrote the following in *Mein Kampf*:

> People who can sneak their way, like parasites, into the human body politic and make others work for them under various pretences can form a State without possessing any definite delimited territory. This is chiefly applicable to that parasitic nation which, particularly at the present time preys upon the honest portion of mankind; I mean the Jews.[129]

Does this sound familiar? It's almost like the Woke Right wolves are getting their talking points straight from this book. Later in *Mein Kampf*, Hitler wrote,

---

[129] Hitler, A. (1939). *Mein Kampf*. Project Gutenberg. (J. Murphy trans.). https://gutenberg.net.au/ebooks02/0200601.txt (Original work published in 1925).

The Jew has never been a nomad, but always a parasite, battening on the substance of others. If he occasionally abandoned regions where he had hitherto lived he did not do it voluntarily. He did it because from time to time he was driven out by people who were tired of having their hospitality abused by such guests. Jewish self-expansion is a parasitic phenomenon—since the Jew is always looking for new pastures for his race.

But this has nothing to do with nomadic life as such; because the Jew does not ever think of leaving a territory which he has once occupied. He sticks where he is with such tenacity that he can hardly be driven out even by superior physical force. He expands into new territories only when certain conditions for his existence are provided therein; but even then—unlike the nomad—he will not change his former abode. He is and remains a parasite, a sponger who, like a pernicious bacillus, spreads over wider and wider areas according as some favourable area attracts him. The effect produced by his presence is also like that of the vampire; for wherever he establishes himself the people who grant him hospitality are bound to be bled to death sooner or later. Thus the Jew has at all times lived in States that have belonged to other races and within the organization of those States he had formed a State of his own, which is, however, hidden behind the mask of a 'religious community', as long as external circumstances do not make it advisable for this community to declare its true nature. As soon as the Jew feels himself sufficiently established in his position to be able to hold it without a disguise, he lifts the mask and suddenly appears in the character which so many did not formerly believe or wish to see: namely that of the Jew.[130]

Furthermore, Hitler stated,

This pestilential adulteration of the blood, of which hundreds of thousands of our people take no account, is being systematically practised by the Jew to-day. Systematically these negroid parasites in our national body corrupt our innocent fair-haired girls and thus destroy something which can no longer be replaced

---

[130] Ibid.

in this world. The two Christian denominations look on with indifference at the profanation and destruction of a noble and unique creature who was given to the world as a gift of God's grace. For the future of the world, however, it does not matter which of the two triumphs over the other, the Catholic or the Protestant. But it does matter whether Aryan humanity survives or perishes.[131]

Hatred of the Jews Leads to Hatred of Christianity

Because true Christianity seeks to protect and show love to the Jews (Romans 9:1-5), Jew-haters and Nazis like Hitler have recognized this fact and fought to oppose the church of God. Another statement which was quoted earlier in this book but which is pertinent here is the following from Michael Spangler:

We anti-Semites are not unmanly. Rather, we are hardened Christian warriors, bound by necessity to fight with all our might against the power of the world, the state, the devil, and indeed the church, all which are sick with godless love for Christ's sworn

---

[131] Ibid.

enemies, the Jews. In this fight we have lost favor, family, friends, work, fellowship, and ministry. And we have done so gladly, for the gain of a clean conscience and the favor of our Lord, and of his faithful servants. This is not at all unmanly.[132]

Because Christianity has inescapably Jewish foundations and eschatology, those who hate the Jews inevitably turn on the church as well. Coincidentally, the previously-mentioned Stephen Wolfe, author of *The Case for Christian Nationalism*, described Spangler as "my friend and a good man"[133] and Wesley Todd, Joel Webbon's co-host, described Spangler as "a faithful minister and Godly man."[134]

When wolves despise the Jews enough, they will always eventually turn on the church. In *Rise of the Aryans: How Ancient Whites Influenced & Established Global*

---

[132] Spangler, M. (2025, March 7). True Manliness and Christian Anti-Semitism. Michael Spangler.
https://spanglermt.substack.com/p/true-manliness-and-christian-anti

[133] Υουκε. (2025, March 8). *Michael is my friend and a good man...* [Image showing a post made by Stephen Wolfe, containing the previous quote]. X.
https://x.com/lagracelaverite/status/1898384141089214701/photo/2

[134] Υουκε. (2025, March 8). *Amen. Don't know him personally but his track record is that of a faithful minister and Godly man...* [Image showing a post made by Wesley Todd, containing the previous quote]. X.
https://x.com/lagracelaverite/status/1898384141089214701/photo/2

Civilization, Patrick Chouinard made the following observation:

> Christianity, at least the one that has existed for more than a century, has been the great enemy of the white race. I see the great monuments and achievements the Church has inspired in our people. In the end, I see even with its putrid connection to diversity and multiculturalism in the name of Christ, I still see the modern Church doing right for the people they serve. But I believe it is now time to sweep away the old order, and put a new one in its place. That can only come from a renewed sense of White Identity. Only by loving the white race with all your heart, mind, soul and strength will the impetus for a drastic change in the plight of our people be achieved. Only then will the true Chosen Race of Nature and the Evolutionary Process, rear up and achieve the greatness it once had. This book is dedicated to those times.[135]

---

[135] Chouinard, P. (2019). *Rise of the Aryans: How Ancient Whites Influenced & Established Global Civilization.* Pp. vii-ix. The Barnes Review History Magazine.

Additionally, Corey Mahler had the following to say about dispensationalist churches:

> Day 1 under Christian Nationalism, we will begin the process of devoting to destruction all false 'houses of worship' — every synagogue, every mosque, every temple, every Palamite or Unitarian or Dispensationalist 'church'.[136]

Brothers and sisters, if what your favorite pastor or podcaster is teaching sounds more like the teaching of Hitler than the teaching of the Bible, you are following a wolf. If he rips the masks off and says that the Jews are "parasites" or that it is now time to fight *the church*, you no longer have any excuse to continue following, defending, and supporting these blind leaders of the blind. If you do so, you are participating in their sin (1 Corinthians 5:11 and 2 John 11) and these malevolent men will drag you to Hell with them. Wake up and free yourself from their cruel grasp; although some of these men may not be fully aware of what they are doing, they are all fighting to win your soul for their Father Below. If you are competent to fight, then expose these

---

[136] Mahler, C. (2025, August 5). *Day 1 under Christian Nationalism, we will begin the process of devoting to destruction all false 'houses of worship' — every...* [Post]. X. https://x.com/CoreyJMahler/status/1952780077747302819

wolves and do not allow them to bring shame on the name of Christ any longer.

We Are All Christ Killers

Those who hate the Jews and who are partial against them will also try to justify their position by claiming that the Jews killed Christ or are "Christ-killers." Before continuing in any kind of conversation along these lines, it is important to ask them, "Are the Jews today genetically descended from the Jews who killed Christ?" Most of them have contradictory beliefs on this question, simultaneously believing that the Jews today are hated by God because they killed Jesus and also believing bizarre, false conspiracies theories that the Jews today are not real Jews, but are European pretenders.

If they do end up acknowledging that the Jews of today are descendants of the same Jews who killed Jesus, they will cite a variety of Bible verses to justify this claim, like Matthew 27:25 and 1 Thessalonians 2:14-16. However, one verse they will *never* cite is Acts 4:27, which says,

> For truly in this city there were gathered together against Your holy servant Jesus, whom You anointed,

both Herod and Pontius Pilate, along with the Gentiles and the peoples of Israel.

It was not only the Israelites who gathered against Jesus and killed Him, but the Gentiles did as well. Thus, a Gentile who calls a Jew a "Christ-killer" is just as much of a "Christ-killer" himself as the Jew is.

The End of Anti-Jewish Partiality

Other than the major excuses already discussed in this book, there are almost an endless number of trivial reasons that Jew-haters have invented to justify their partiality against what Romans 11:28 describes as God's chosen people. They claim the Jews are plotting world domination by controlling mass media, governments, and banks; the Jews created Communism (never mind that a Jewish woman attempted to assassinate Lenin and that Jews were relentlessly persecuted in the Soviet Union); the Jews cause pandemics; the Jews are a "pernicious threat" to Christianity (despite the fact that there are many Messianic Jews who practice Judaism and are Christians); the Jews steal Christian children and consume their blood at Passover; the Jews run the porn industry; the Jews fabricated or exaggerated the Holocaust to make White people feel bad for them; the Jews are evil for controlling the Atlantic slave trade (even though this slave trade is documented to have been controlled almost exclusively by Whites); the Jews poison and fill up the wells of White people; the Jews were behind the September 11, 2001 terrorist attacks (disregard the fact that hundreds of Jews died in the attacks and thousands signed up with the U.S. military to fight those who were responsible); the Jews destroy the homes of White people with space lasers; and the list goes on and on. Satan never tires of creating lies to justify his evil deeds, and, one of the evil deeds he is most passionate about is his attempt to exterminate the Jews.

Christians are sternly warned not to behave arrogantly towards the Israelites. Romans 11:18-22 states,

> Do not be arrogant toward the branches; but if you are arrogant, remember that it is not you who supports the root, but the root supports you. You will say then, "Branches were broken off so that I might be grafted in." Quite right, they were broken off for their unbelief, but you stand by your faith. Do not be conceited, but fear; for if God did not spare the

natural branches, He will not spare you, either. Behold then the kindness and severity of God; to those who fell, severity, but to you, God's kindness, if you continue in His kindness; otherwise you also will be cut off.

Romans 11:26 reaffirms that God still has a plan for Israel and that the whole nation will be saved. Meanwhile, Romans 11:28-29 remind us,

From the standpoint of the gospel they [the Jews] are enemies for your sake, but from the standpoint of God's choice they are beloved for the sake of the fathers; for the gifts and the calling of God are irrevocable.

Despite what the Jew-hating conspiracy theorists claim, the Jews do not currently rule the world. They are currently one of the smallest and most hated peoples on the earth. But one day, a Jew will rule the world from Israel. Then, at that time, the Bible promises that all the Gentiles of the world will finally serve the Jews. No more anti-Jewish partiality will be allowed. Zechariah 8:22-23 promises,

"So many peoples and mighty nations will come to seek the LORD of hosts in Jerusalem and to entreat the favor of the LORD." Thus says the LORD of hosts, "In those days ten men from all the nations will grasp the garment of a Jew, saying, 'Let us go with you, for we have heard that God is with you.'"

Isaiah 49:14-16 says,

But Zion said, "The LORD has forsaken me, and the Lord has forgotten me." Can a woman forget her nursing child and have no compassion on the son of her womb? Even these may forget, but I will not forget you. Behold, I have inscribed you on the palms of My hands; Your walls are continually before Me.

Shortly after this, verses 22-23 reveal,

Thus says the Lord GOD, "Behold, I will lift up My hand to the nations and set up My standard to the peoples; and they will bring your sons in their bosom, and your daughters will be carried on their shoulders. Kings will be your guardians, and their princesses your nurses. They will bow down to you with their faces to the earth and lick the dust of your feet; and you will know that I am the LORD; those who hopefully wait for Me will not be put to shame."

A little bit after this, verse 26 gives a frightful warning to those who dare to oppress the children of Israel:

> I will feed your [Israel's] oppressors with their own flesh, and they will become drunk with their own blood as with sweet wine; and all flesh will know that I, the LORD, am your Savior and your Redeemer, the Mighty One of Jacob.

I will conclude this section with selected verses from Isaiah 60 (verses 1-5, 10-16, and 20-22), which is one of the most glorious prophecies about the blessings of God on Israel during the Millennial Reign, which is soon to come to pass:

> Arise, shine; for your [Israel's] light has come, and the glory of the LORD has risen upon you. For behold, darkness will cover the earth and deep darkness the peoples; but the LORD will rise upon you and His glory will appear upon you. Nations will come to your light, and kings to the brightness of your rising. Lift up your eyes round about and see; they all gather together, they come to you. Your sons will come from afar, and your daughters will be carried in the arms. Then you will see and be radiant,

and your heart will thrill and rejoice; because the abundance of the sea will be turned to you, the wealth of the nations will come to you. [...]

Foreigners will build up your walls, and their kings will minister to you; for in My wrath I struck you, and in My favor I have had compassion on you. Your gates will be open continually; they will not be closed day or night, so that men may bring to you the wealth of the nations, with their kings led in procession. For the nation and the kingdom which will not serve you will perish, and the nations will be utterly ruined. The glory of Lebanon will come to you, the juniper, the box tree and the cypress together, to beautify the place of My sanctuary; and I shall make the place of My feet glorious. The sons of those who afflicted you will come bowing to you, and all those who despised you will bow themselves at the soles of your feet; And they will call you the city of the LORD, the Zion of the Holy One of Israel. Whereas you have been forsaken and hated with no one passing through, I will make you an everlasting pride, a joy from generation to generation. You will also suck the milk of nations and suck the breast of kings; then you will know that I, the LORD, am your Savior and your Redeemer, the Mighty One of Jacob. [...]

Your sun will no longer set, nor will your moon wane; for you will have the LORD for an everlasting light, and the days of your mourning will be over. Then all your people will be righteous; they will possess the land forever, the branch of My planting, the work of My hands, that I may be glorified. The smallest one will become a clan, and the least one a mighty nation. I, the LORD, will hasten it in its time.

Even so, come *Yeshua Hamashiach*! Hasten Your return and rescue the nation and people of Israel from all those who afflict her and despise her, for the sake of Your covenant with their fathers. Let all those who hate the Jews and the Israelites be put to shame, for You are mighty and will bring to pass all the glorious things that you have prophesied.

The Swastika in the Sanctuary

The Swastika in the Sanctuary

Chapter V: Holocaust Denial

In an interesting exchange where a self-described "Reich Wing Radical" influencer was presented with evidence that Anne Frank (a Jewish girl who was murdered in the Holocaust) was a real person who really did write the diary entries attributed to her, he responded,

> Honestly I don't care if her account is real or not, if people believing it is fake makes them antisemitic I'm going to spread that it is fake.[137]

The motive expressed in this statement is also the standard motive for many who deny the Holocaust. However, very few Holocaust deniers are as honest about their motives as this influencer.

It is a strange reality that we are witnessing: today's Neo-Nazis are simultaneously proud of what Germany did to the Jews and will argue that it was justified, while also denying that the Holocaust happened. Sometimes, a

---

[137] Esoteric Spooklerist. (2025, August 25). *Honestly I don't care if her account is real or not, if people believing it is fake makes them antisemitic...* [Post]. X.
https://x.com/RadSpooklerist/status/1960020376303333567

Neo-Nazi will flip back and forth between these positions in a matter of minutes during an argument. In so doing, these Neo-Nazis display the conflicting pride and guilty conscience of a serial killer. On one hand, they are proud of the evil things they have done and advocated for, and crave acknowledgement from others. On the other hand, they are deeply ashamed of their wicked deeds and beliefs, and desperately try to cover up their sins.

Is Denying the Holocaust a Sin?

Holocaust denial is being pushed and protected by today's Nazi-sympathizers, who are causing this sin to proliferate in the church. But is it really sinful to deny that the Holocaust happened? Is it actually wrong to deny that a historical event happened? The short answer to these questions is "yes"; it is sinful to lie about something which happened in history and to bear false witness against your neighbors (even those who are long dead) by claiming that what they witnessed did not happen.

The Holocaust is one of the most well-documented events in history and millions of eyewitnesses (victims, perpetrators, and other observers), including many faithful

Christian saints, testified that it happened. If someone denies that the Holocaust happened, he has no reason to believe that any other historical event happened, since very few (if any) have had as much evidence supporting them as the Holocaust. If someone acknowledges that Alexander the Great existed or that George Washington crossed the Delaware River, but denies that the Holocaust happened, he is guilty of the sin of hypocrisy, since there is much more evidence for the Holocaust than these other two events of history which he accepts.

If someone denies that the Holocaust happened, chalking up the millions of eyewitness accounts, physical evidence, and documents to a massive conspiracy, he must be consistent and apply this same standard to every other event of history. Put into practice, this would cause him to become an agnostic about the historicity of every other event that he did not personally see with his eyes. If he is not consistent with this standard and behaves hypocritically, it shows that he has some agenda for denying the overwhelming evidence for the Holocaust while accepting lesser amounts of evidence for other events of history.

The Word of God has a lot to say about liars and those who bear false witness against their neighbors. Exodus 20:16 explicitly states, "You shall not bear false witness against your neighbor," with no qualifications given. The command gives no leeway to make up categories of neighbors who it is okay to lie about, such as those who are dead or those who you do not know personally. Proverbs 12:22 says that "lying lips are an abomination to the LORD" and Proverbs 6:17 lists "a lying tongue" as one of seven things that God hates and that are an abomination to Him, in the same list as "hands that shed innocent blood".

Proverbs 12:19 promises, "Truthful lips will be established forever, but a lying tongue is only for a moment." Proverbs 19:5 warns, "A false witness will not go unpunished, and he who tells lies will not escape." Likewise, Proverbs 19:9 warns that false witnesses and liars will die for their unrepentant sin when it says, "A false witness will not go unpunished, and he who tells lies will perish." Psalm 101:7 says, "He who practices deceit shall not dwell within my house; he who speaks falsehood shall not maintain his position before me."

In the New Testament, Colossians 3:9 and Ephesians 4:25 instruct us to stop lying to each other and to only speak truth instead. Revelation 21:8 warns that *all* unrepentant liars will be sentenced to a second death in the lake of fire. And Revelation 22:15 adds, "Outside are the dogs and the sorcerers and the immoral persons and the murderers and the idolaters, and everyone who loves and practices lying."

After reading all these verses, how can any Christian ever make the claim that it is fine to lie about the Holocaust? The Bible describes those who practice lying in the same way that it describes the very worst of evils, including murder, and promises that those who make a practice of this, if they do not repent, will be sentenced to Hell.

The Historicity of the Holocaust

At this point, some readers may ask for specific evidence which supports the historicity of the Holocaust since, of course, if the Holocaust did not happen, Holocaust deniers are not lying. Although it is beyond the scope of this book to provide all of the documentation and eyewitness accounts of the Holocaust or to refute all of the specific claims of Holocaust deniers, many excellent resources are available to those who want to go deeper than surface level.

I highly recommend Shermer and Grobman's *Denying History: Who Says the Holocaust Never Happened and Why Do They Say It?*; Evans' *Lying About Hitler*; and Jan van Pelt's *The Case for Auschwitz: Evidence from the Irving Trial*. These works do an excellent job of specifically answering historical objections and theories presented by Holocaust deniers.

For thorough, well-researched books explaining the history of the Holocaust and providing documentary evidence for it, I suggest reading Gilbert's *The Holocaust: A History of the Jews of Europe During the Second World War* and Funnel, Bigoni, and Twyford's fascinating new book *Accounting for the Holocaust: Enabling the Final Solution.*

A book which gives the first-hand witness of a remarkable saint of God who saved Jews from the Holocaust is Ten Boom's *The Hiding Place*. Lastly, a book which gives the testimony of hundreds of Nazi murderers and which is one of the best books of all time, in my opinion, is Browning's *Ordinary Men: Reserve Police Battalion 101 and the Final Solution in Poland.*

Truly, it would not take "ten thousand hours" to learn the truth about the number of Jews killed in the Holocaust, like Joel Webbon has claimed.[138] A few days (or, for those wanting to be very thorough, a week or a month) of reading some of these resources, combined with basic critical thinking skills, is all that it would take to establish that the Holocaust really did happen and that the estimated numbers are more likely than not to be true.

But, if someone did want to spend "ten thousand hours" studying the minutiae of the Holocaust to supplement the major points of evidence available in the resources which I listed, they could do so. There are almost innumerable accounts from eyewitnesses, scientists, and historicists which provide testimony about the Holocaust. The same cannot be said for the Holocaust-denial camp, which has very few primary sources and accounts which they allege support their position.

Interestingly, Webbon apparently found the "ten thousand hours" needed to calculate the minimum number of German civilian deaths after World War II:

---

[138] Right Response Ministries. (2024, October 2). *When A Member In Our Church Shared A Holocaust Meme* [Video]. YouTube. https://www.youtube.com/watch?v=pj7L7b66xLY&t=5063s

After Germany lost WW2, well over a million German civilians (including women and children) were raped and murdered while America's military and politicians looked on. America has been taught for 80 years that we were the virtuous heroes in that war. Therefore, America's leaders will blindly side with Israel, thinking itself virtuous once again as Israel slaughters Palestinians.[139]

Certainly, many German civilians were killed at the hands of the Soviets during and after World War II, although it is unclear where Webbon found the number he cited. I am not saying that this atrocity described by Webbon did not happen and I fully recognize that the Communists did horrible things during their reign. However, there is a double standard here that serves as a perfect example of the type of hypocrisy and partiality that is shown by many wolves in regard to the Holocaust.

When it comes to the Holocaust, a tragedy that they *don't* want to acknowledge (because it makes their ideology unattractive to normal people), they show great skepticism,

---

[139] Webbon, J. (2025, August 23). *Yes, @RepMTG This is why history matters. After Germany lost WW2, well over a million German civilians (including women and...* [Post]. X. https://x.com/rightresponsem/status/1959305589814652934

even though there is significant evidence that the event occurred and that the numbers are likely to be correct. When it comes to other tragedies that they *do* want to acknowledge (because they make their ideology more attractive to normal people), they will happily repeat specific information about that tragedy they learned from an anonymous person online, doing only the most cursory of research, if any. If they refuse to accept the mountains of evidence for the Holocaust, on what grounds do they accept lesser evidence for any other atrocity? Wolves who do this type of thing flagrantly exhibit their sins of hypocrisy and partiality for all to see.

Just Asking Questions?

Some wolves would object to the things that I have said so far here by saying, "I'm just asking questions! There isn't anything wrong with that." If it is true that someone is strictly just asking questions, I agree with this statement. There is nothing wrong with questioning historical reports and desiring to know the truth—in fact, this is a very good thing. However, many of the people who claim that they are "just asking questions" go further than questioning and make definitive statements (or statements which unmistakably imply) that the Holocaust did not happen. This is lying.

An Alternative View of History?

Others will say that there is nothing inherently wrong with holding to an "alternative view of history" (that is, a view or belief about a historical event that is not mainstream). I also agree that it is not *inherently* wrong to have an alternative view of history. The only thing that matters is whether or not the alternative view is true or not. The opinion of the masses does not matter in establishing whether or not something is true. In the specific case of the Holocaust, the alternative view is not true, so this objection is not relevant.

"But, I don't think it can ever be wrong for someone to hold to an alternative view of history. Surely you're not going to tell me that those who believe the Moon landing was fake, that JFK was killed by the CIA, or that the September 11th terrorist attacks were an inside job are sinning, are you?" This is a very common objection presented by Holocaust deniers (or those who are sympathetic to this sin). It is foolish to make a statement like this; although it is designed purely to protect the pet sin of Holocaust denial, it has very broad reaching, unintended implications. If it can't be wrong for someone to hold to an "alternative view of history," there is nothing wrong with a professor who teaches his students that the Communists never starved to death millions of people, which can be easily proven false.

This example may be objected to by those who are sympathetic to Holocaust deniers by saying, "Well the real reason why it is wrong for someone to hold to this alternative view of history is that this person is probably a Leftist, socialist, or Communist, and that is why they are telling this lie." I would first respond to this by saying that there are many Bible verses which indicate that lying is evil without adding the stipulation "but only if you have evil motivations."

There are a few passages which imply that it is good to lie to save the innocent from death (Exodus 1:19-20, Joshua 2:4, James 2:25, and Hebrews 11:31), but this is the only time lying is ever approved of in the Word of God. Those who lie about Communist and Nazi atrocities are not lying to save the innocent from death and there is nothing in

Scripture which indicates that it is okay to lie "just for kicks" as long as you don't have any evil intentions. But I would further respond to this objection by saying that Holocaust deniers *almost always* are Nazi-sympathizers or are partial against the Jews. This is obvious to anyone who has observed or been around Holocaust deniers. It is equally as obvious that a Holocaust denier is lying for these reasons as it is that the professor denies Communist atrocities because he is Leftist, socialist, or Communist.

Additionally, if it is acceptable for people to believe and teach lies about history, what other areas of study would this apply to? What if someone has an "alternative view" of biology? If someone believes that it is possible for a male to have a vagina, why is that wrong? After all, the Bible doesn't explicitly say that a man can't have a vagina, so you can't object to this claim on purely Biblical grounds.

What if someone's "alternative view" of biology says that human life doesn't begin until birth? Can that be wrong? What if someone's "alternative view" of health science teaches that ingesting dishwasher pods is healthy for you? On what grounds could you say that he was wrong? Since he just has an "alternative view," it must be fine. What if someone's "alternative view" of economics says that a government can print as much money as it wants with no consequences? Is this person actually doing anything wrong when he advises lawmakers to turn on the printing presses because of this "alternative view" which he holds? Clearly, believing the truth about things is important, so this "alternative view" nonsense needs to stop.

What about those who believe that the September 11th terrorist attacks were an inside job (or similar conspiracy theories or alternative views of history)? In this case, the amount of evidence suggesting that the attacks were carried out by the U.S. government is paltry compared to overwhelming weight of evidence which indicates the Holocaust happened. Anyone who believes that the September 11th attacks were an inside job while denying that the Holocaust happened demonstrates his hypocrisy.

However, if the terrorist attacks were truly an inside job, it would be sinful for government officials to lie to the public and teach a different view or theory other than what really happened. If you don't believe it is wrong to lie or hold "alternative views" about historical events, you have no moral grounds to be opposed to government officials who you believe lied about the terror attacks. But if it is sinful for these government officials to lie and present an alternative view about what really happened regarding these attacks, then it logically follows that it is sinful for people to lie and present an alternative view about the Holocaust as well.

There are certainly many events in history where there is minimal evidence of what really happened presently available and, because of this, competing theories and views have arisen. In such cases where the truth cannot be confidently known, it is imperative that we do not overstate what we believe happened. It is fine to create theories about these events, as long as you remain open-minded and willing to change your views, listen to criticism from others, and present your theories to others with humility. It is sinful, however, to lie by saying or implying that your view of a historical event is certainly correct when there is not sufficient evidence to support your position. New evidence may eventually prove your theory to be correct, but in the meantime you do not have an excuse to dogmatically and confidently assert whatever you want as if it was a fact. Without sufficient evidence to support your claim, as far as you are aware, you are telling a lie.

Apart from the sinfulness of it, it is also wise not to engage in this type of behavior for the sake of your own reputation. In many cases, your theories will be proven false shortly and you will be humiliated in front of those you overconfidently presented your theory to. For example, conservatives who confidently stated that Patriot Front was run by Biden's federal law enforcement agencies to make Republicans look bad were humiliated as this lie was exposed in front of everyone after Trump entered office and Patriot Front kept doing the same things. So, in regards to historical events where there is minimal information available, it is best to remain somewhat open-minded and to never be too emphatic that your theory is true.

However, none of this applies to historical events where the significant amount of evidence is sufficient to establish that it happened or that a specific view of the event is correct. In such cases, which includes the Holocaust, denying that the event happened or proposing an alternative view which is not true is sinful because it is lying. There is simply no way that a Christian can, in good conscience and without hypocrisy, approve of lying about history.

The Purpose of Lies

The primary weapon in Satan's arsenal is deception. Lies exist to justify perversion, murder, and every kind of evil, as well as to cover up the evil deeds of fallen men and angels. Satan and the gullible fools who listen to him used lies to justify the Holocaust and, even to this day, use lies in an attempt to cover it up. Those who propagate Holocaust denial are helping the mass murderer, Satan, conceal his evil deeds and, because of this, are aiding and abetting his crimes. As Christians, we must thoroughly root out all lies which wolves in the church have attempted to spread. This certainly includes Holocaust denial.

Holocaust denial, justification, and the other lies which they tell about the Jews are being used by Satan in preparation for his next attempt at a Holocaust. Aleksandr Solzhenitsyn, author of *The Gulag Archipelago*, a three-volume non-fiction series about the horrors of the Soviet gulags, made the following statement in a speech after receiving the Nobel Prize in Literature:

> [...] Let us not forget that violence does not and cannot exist by itself. It is invariably intertwined with the lie. They are linked in the most intimate, most

organic and profound fashion. Violence cannot
conceal itself behind anything except lies, and lies
have nothing to maintain them save violence. Anyone
who has once proclaimed violence as his method
must inexorably choose the lie as his principle. [...]
Violence [does not] always and necessarily lunge
straight for your throat; more often than not it
demands of its subjects only that they pledge
allegiance to lies, that they participate in falsehood.
The simple act of an ordinary brave man is not to
participate in lies, not to support false actions! His
rule: let that come into the world, let it even reign
supreme—only not through me.[140]

---

[140] Solzhenitsyn, A. (n.d.). Notable Quotations. The Aleksandr
Solzhenitsyn Center.
https://www.solzhenitsyncenter.org/notable-quotations

The Swastika in the Sanctuary

Chapter VI: The Antioch Solution

You would think it should go without saying that it is essential for competent Christians, who know the Bible well and who have love, wisdom, patience, and self-control, to confront wolves who are threatening the flock, including today's wolves who teach Nazi false doctrines. Unsurprisingly, however, many wolves in the church are spreading the lie that some people should not be opposed.

No More Brother Wars

These wolves use a variety of slogans to proscribe calling out heretics who are "on our side" politically, including "no enemies to the right (NETTR)," "no enemies on the Right (NEOTR)," and "no more brother wars." Interestingly, this last slogan originated with White supremacists who used it to describe the need for White nations to stop fighting each other, claiming it is Jews who instigate conflict between White brothers.[141] Certain wolves

---

[141] No More Brother Wars. (n.d.). Hatepedia, produced by the Online Hate Research and Education Project, which is an initiative of The

in the church repurposed the term to refer to no more brother wars between any men who are on the Right or, depending on who you ask, any men who are on the Right and who claim to be Christians.

These slogans and beliefs are idiotic, illogical, and downright dangerous. "No enemies to the right" is particularly dangerous, because it results in ever increasing radicalization, the same thing that has happened to the Left over the last several decades. If you cannot criticize people who are *to the right* of you politically, but they can criticize you because you are to the left of them, they will gain more adherents. After all, they are allowed to point out how bad your position is, but they are exempt from criticism. This creates a situation where the people who are the farthest to the right politically are, effectively, members of a privileged class which cannot be criticized by anyone.

Anyone daring to challenge these cool guys is branded as a "Liberal" or a "Leftist," and for this reason alone, their criticisms are disregarded. This foolish concept, promoted by many wolves, is one of the primary reasons

---

Toronto Holocaust Museum.
https://hatepedia.ca/guide/explicit/no-more-brother-wars-no-more-brothe
rs-wars

why so many young men, in particular, are starting to openly refer to themselves as Nazis. Currently, that is as far right as you can go. Like Antifa kids on the Left, Nazi kids on the Right are protected from any criticism and are peak cool.

Wolves who are slightly more sophisticated will only use the slogans "no enemies on the right" and "no more brother wars." But both of these terms are also highly problematic and unbiblical. Pastor Doug Wilson wisely observed the danger posed from this type of thinking in the following statement:

A number of Christian conservatives are acting as though they will have no enemies to the right, and that is why they will never "punch right." All this does is tell the devil to make sure he comes after their soul from the right. "Hey, devil! This flank is completely exposed! I trust you will be a gentleman about it!"

Always remember that he is smarter than you are, and astonishingly cruel. After you have been in Hell for ten thousand years, it will be small consolation to you that when you tumbled headlong into the Abyss you were on the right wing of that column of souls that rushed over the lip.

Hard words? If they hurt, just ignore them. You are already ignoring harder words.[142]

This exemption of criticism for the Right is idolatrous. The only person we can never criticize is God, because He is the only being who is perfect. If someone gives this privilege to anything else, that is his god. If his refusal to criticize the Right causes him to refuse to save souls from the clutches of wolves who are leading them into sin, like God commands him to if he is capable of doing so (Galatians 6:1, Jude 23, and James 5:20), then he has chosen to put his love for the Right above his love for God and his neighbor.

If someone is a seeker-sensitive pastor on the Right who refuses to call out the sins of Nazi wolves who are ravaging his flock, simply because they are on the Right, then he is failing at his job as a shepherd. He will give an account to God for the souls of his flock (Hebrews 13:7). What will he do when he stands before God and is asked

---

[142] Wilson, D. (2023, April 24). Ethnic Conceit as Denial of Christ. Blog & Mablog.
https://dougwils.com/books-and-culture/s7-engaging-the-culture/ethnic-conceit-as-denial-of-christ.html

why he allowed his sheep to believe and teach others that the Jews are parasites and deserved to be killed in the Holocaust, that Jesus was not a Jew, and that the God of the Old Testament is actually Satan?

Most importantly, however, the claim that certain political groups are off-limits for criticism is contradicted by the Bible. 1 Timothy 5:20 states, "Those who continue in sin, rebuke in the presence of all, so that the rest also will be fearful of sinning." Some who don't want to call out wolves on the Right excuse their actions by claiming, "If we call out that guy, his platform will only get even more attention." But this verse contradicts that claim. Paul explicitly tells Timothy, a pastor, to call out unrepentant wolves publicly so that others will be afraid of sinning.

Ephesians 5:11-13 also warns,

Do not participate in the unfruitful deeds of darkness, but instead even expose them; for it is disgraceful even to speak of the things which are done by them in secret. But all things become visible when they are exposed by the light, for everything that becomes visible is light.

We are explicitly instructed to publicly expose the sinful words and actions of wolves, especially if they are secret or have been covered up, so that their sins can be brought to light. For the light to do its disinfecting work, their sins must be exposed publicly. Do not allow wolves to emotionally manipulate you into keeping their sinful words and actions private.

Must Your Rebuke of Nazis Only Be Private?

But what about Matthew 18:15-17, which says that you should confront someone who sins privately before bringing it to the attention of the whole church? Clearly, this passage is referring to private sins which are committed by normal churchgoers who do not have a public ministry and which do not present a significant threat to others. For example, if someone at your church is rude to you, Matthew 18:15-17 must be followed.

However, some twist Matthew 18:15-17 to imply it is wrong to publicly call out a right-wing podcaster or pastor who is teaching or doing sinful things without discussing your differences with him privately in the "DM's" first. Even apart from the Biblical issues with this, there are some huge logical problems to deal with.

If a pastor is convicted of sexually abusing a minor, do you have to contact him in prison and discuss your differences with him before you warn others that he is a wolf, per Matthew 18? If you disagree with a dead heretic in the church, like Marcion, are you forbidden from warning others that he was a wolf, because it is not possible for you to confront him privately, per Matthew 18? If a wolf on the Left who you have never met before but who has a very large ministry teaches that Communism is compatible with the Bible, do you have to reach out to him privately before warning others about his false teaching publicly, per Matthew 18? If you answer, "No, because he is on the Left," then I will ask, "Where does Matthew 18 distinguish between Right and Left when it comes to how you handle church discipline?"

The Antioch Solution

Biblically, it is not only permissible, but also required for us to publicly expose and call out the private and public sins of those who threaten the church, if we are capable of doing so. There is no requirement for a wolf to be confronted privately first. One of the best examples of this is found in Galatians 2:11-14, the story of Paul and Peter in Antioch:

> But when Cephas [Peter] came to Antioch, I opposed him to his face, because he stood condemned. For prior to the coming of certain men from James, he used to eat with the Gentiles; but when they came, he began to withdraw and hold himself aloof, fearing the party of the circumcision. The rest of the Jews joined him in hypocrisy, with the result that even Barnabas was carried away by their hypocrisy. But when I saw that they were not straightforward about the truth of the gospel, I said to Cephas in the presence of all, "If you, being a Jew, live like the Gentiles and not like the Jews, how is it that you compel the Gentiles to live like Jews?"

Notice that Paul was not obligated to talk to Peter privately about his hypocrisy before calling him out in front of everyone. Also, remember that Peter was a great apostle, the rock on which the church was built (Matthew 16:18), who later went on to write two books of the Bible. If Paul could call out Peter for his sin publicly (even sins which some Christians on the Right would not think were that big of deal, like hypocrisy, racial partiality, and not being "straightforward about the truth of the Gospel"), then truly no one is off-limits for criticism. Peter was on Paul's "team," but that didn't remove Paul's responsibility to speak out against his sin publicly. And, compared to the sins of actual wolves today (like those committed by the Neo-Nazis, Marcionites, and the teachers who ally themselves with them and shield them from criticism), Peter's sins were very trivial. So, we should certainly condemn the degeneracy of wolves who are exceedingly sinful today.

Do not Associate With nazis

As has been mentioned earlier in this book, we are also instructed not to associate with any person who claims to be a Christian but who lives a lifestyle characterized by gross sin. In 1 Corinthians 5:9-13, Paul states,

> I wrote you in my letter not to associate with immoral people; I did not at all mean with the immoral people of this world, or with the covetous and swindlers, or with idolaters, for then you would have to go out of the world. But actually, I wrote to you not to

associate with any so-called brother if he is an immoral person, or covetous, or an idolater, or a reviler, or a drunkard, or a swindler—not even to eat with such a one. For what have I to do with judging outsiders? Do you not judge those who are within the church? But those who are outside, God judges. Remove the wicked man from among yourselves.

This passage alone disproves the idea of NETTR, NEOTR, and "no more brother wars." As Christians, we are explicitly instructed to remove ourselves from association with any grossly sinful person who claims to be a Christian, even if he also claims to be on our political team. If a so-called "Christian" lives a life characterized by his unrepentant love for the Nazis (one of the most satanic political movements that ever existed), by bearing false witness against the Jews (e.g., denying the Holocaust, claiming that the Jews of today are not real Jews but are European pretenders, or saying that the Jews run the world), or by reviling (directing foul language, slander, or angry outbursts at others), then Christians *cannot* associate with him. We cannot even have a meal with such a person, let alone invite them to speak at our conferences or defend them on social media. Those who do these things are disobeying God, even if they try to excuse themselves by saying that the sinful "Christians" they are associating with are on their political team.

Restore the One Caught in Nazism

Lastly, a point which was alluded to previously is that capable Christians are obligated to attempt to save the souls of other Christians who are being led astray by wolves. Galatians 6:1 says,

> Brethren, even if anyone is caught in any trespass, you who are spiritual, restore such a one in a spirit of gentleness; each one looking to yourself, so that you too will not be tempted.

A similar command is found in Jude 23, which states, "save others, snatching them out of the fire; and on some have mercy with fear, hating even the garment polluted by the flesh." For those who succeed in doing this, James 5:20 comments, "let him know that he who turns a sinner from the error of his way will save his soul from death and will cover a multitude of sins."

If you see a friend or family member fanboying over the teachings of a wolf, you need to warn him and try to stop him from going down a path designed by Satan to result in the destruction of his soul. If you are a pastor and you learn that a group of young men in your church are excitedly discussing the cool things they have learned from a "Christian" podcast which sympathizes with the Nazis and teaches their doctrines, you need to be a man, speak to them, and put a stop to this cancer before it spreads in your church.

To confront these individuals and try to save their souls from death, you must be willing to say that a wolf is a wolf, even if you consider him to be on your political team. When you attempt to save others from death like this, you must be very careful to guard your own soul. Almost certainly, your friends, family members, and church acquaintances you attempt to save will tempt you with arguments for the sinful lifestyle and worldview that they have come to adopt. You must be mentally strong, refuse their seductive temptations, and hate the wicked things they are attracted to.

Most importantly, in this battle which you may face, you must remain immersed in the Word of God. Do not be partial to the Right or Left, since both sides will lie to you and attempt to make you swerve from the path of life. Instead, let God be your only loyalty and His Word your highest source of wisdom, lest you be tempted by the enemy. In this noble endeavor, ensure that Proverbs 4:20-27 is your constant meditation:

> My son, give attention to my words; incline your ear to my sayings. Do not let them depart from your sight; keep them in the midst of your heart. For they are life to those who find them and health to all their body. Watch over your heart with all diligence, for from it flow the springs of life. Put away from you a deceitful mouth and put devious speech far from you. Let your eyes look directly ahead and let your gaze be fixed straight in front of you. Watch the path of your feet and all your ways will be established. Do not turn to the right nor to the left; turn your foot from evil.

www.ingramcontent.com/pod-product-compliance
Lightning Source LLC
Chambersburg PA
CBHW031155270326
41931CB00006B/286